Rule the Night – Win the Fight
A Practical Guide to Low-Light Gun Fighting

Edward M. Santos

Rule the Night – Win the Fight
A Practical Guide to Low-Light Gun Fighting

By Edward M. Santos

First Edition

Copyright © 2007 Tactical Services Press

ISBN: 978-0-9796690-0-2
Printed in the United States of America

Published by Tactical Services Press, a division of
Center Target Sports, Inc.
PO Box 2487
Hayden, Idaho 83835

Direct inquiries and/or orders to the above address or
Contact us online at: www.tacticalservices.com

Cover photo by Frank Martin
Frank Martin Photography
All photographs and illustrations by the author unless otherwise noted.

Dedication

To my wife, Peggy, the ultimate partner, wife and best friend. A special thank you for all your time spent proof reading, not to mention your vision, guidance, determination, and tenacity.

I Love You…

Table of contents

FOREWORD

I was flattered that spring day at the ILEETA (International Law Enforcement Educators and Trainers Association) conference when Ed Santos invited me to write this foreword for *Rule the Night and Win the Fight*. The topic of this book has been an ongoing passion of mine for decades. We have long known that most gunfights take place under less than perfect lighting conditions...and that our species is not at its most comfortable when we can't see perfectly.

I was reminded of a cartoon in a police professional journal, back in the '70s or so. (I want to say it appeared in either "Trooper" or "Law and Order".) A state police supervisor is speaking sternly to a trooper. The trooper is wearing a Dracula cape over his uniform, and is sporting vampire fangs. "Ed," the supervisor is saying, "I think you've been on midnights too long."

Now, the Ed who wrote this book is too young to be that Ed, but the old cartoon is still on point to the topic at hand. Human beings are diurnal creatures, not nocturnal. We are not comfortable in the dark, and those who seem too comfortable lurking in the gloom make the rest of us nervous. Note that the first tools early Man seems to have harnessed were weapons (homo sapiens is the tool-bearing mammal and, therefore, the weapon-bearing mammal), and fire. The fire was not just to ward off the cold and cook our food. It served to illuminate the darkness. Weapons and illumination brought our kind to the top of the food chain and to the rule of the planet. In treating them as he does here, at the most advanced state of their evolution in tandem with one another, Ed Santos does us all an important service.

Ed has studied these related topics deeply and to the edge of the present state of their art, and more important, has distilled those studies into this handy and most useful compendium. Not all of us in the business agree on every subtlety of the use of illumination in danger situations – if we did, a group such as ILEETA or IALEFI, the International Association of Law Enforcement Firearms Instructors, would be a mutual admiration society, not a forum for advancement of disciplines that encompass relevant arts and sciences. For instance, I agree with author Santos that the strobing effect introduced by Ken Goode and embodied in the trend-setting Gladius light from Blackhawk has enormous potential when dealing with hostile individuals in the dark. However, I noticed that the same strobe effect that disorients the suspect also makes it more difficult for the good guy to watch that person's hands. Solution: using the street-proven Contact and Cover principle brilliantly conceived by John Morrison and his colleagues at the San Diego Police Department, have the Contact officer put the strobing beam in the suspect's eyes, while the Cover officer puts a solid beam of light on the area of the suspect's hands. As Ed Santos says, "More than likely, you will pick a few techniques that work for your style, practice them, modify them as needed, perfect them and I hope by all means use and share them."

Don't just read Ed's book, absorb it. It stands at the cutting edge of this fast-developing area of knowledge right now. The advice it contains can keep good people alive. It's important.

FOREWORD

Ed is right when he says those who have the tools and tactics to win the fight in the dark will rule the night. All I can add is he who controls the light need not fear the darkness.

Stay safe,

Massad Ayoob
July 2007

Massad Ayoob served 20 years as chair of the firearms committee of ASLET, the American Society of Law Enforcement Trainers, and founded the Lethal Force Institute in 1981 and has served as its director ever since. He works full time researching and teaching use of force and management of violent encounters, and part time as a fully sworn police officer with command rank over full time personnel. Ayoob was voted by his peers the Outstanding American Handgunner of the Year in 1998, and in 1996 received the National Tactical Advocate award.

Edward M. Santos, owner and founder of Center Target Sports, Inc. has been teaching firearms and defensive tactics for over 25 years. He is a retired Army officer and has been a certified Level One Reserve Deputy in North Idaho for over 9 years. He is recognized in the Idaho court system as a firearms expert witness.

Through Center Target Sports and Tactical Services Group (a division of CTS, Inc), he teaches the latest, cutting edge defensive skills, techniques, and concepts to law enforcement, civilians and armed professionals across the country and internationally.

His years of experience in the military as well as law enforcement have allowed him to gain first hand knowledge of high stress lethal encounters. Ed is a dedicated, demanding instructor who has never ceased to be the student as well. He has pursued both basic and advanced courses in the fields of professional firearms training and education.

To this end he has attended courses at many recognized police and private firearms training academies to include the Idaho Police Officers Standards and Training (POST), Washington State Criminal Justice Training Commission, Alameda County (California) Sheriff's Office Regional Training Center, Burbank (California) Police Department, Las Vegas (Nevada) Police Department, Steele Foundation, Chapman Academy, Rogers Shooting School, SureFire Academy, FirstLight Incorporated, Taser International, Monadnock, and many others.

He has been awarded instructor-level status from the NRA, Idaho POST, Washington State Criminal Justice .Training

---

Commission, SureFire Academy, FirstLight Inc., Taser International, Monadnock, TMA Safe Police Systems, and Specialized Training Consultants.

He is passionate about exploring, understanding and controlling the Low-light environment we so often have to operate in. He has developed a number of innovative teaching techniques and exercises which facilitate his students' understanding of Low-light theories and tactics.

Ed has consulted with light manufacturers and designed a number of very popular tactical and personal defense lighting systems. He continues to experiment with new technologies and materials, and clinical research in an effort to improve on the light systems currently available in our industry. Performance, dependability and affordability are always at the root of his designs and innovations.

ACKNOWLEDGEMENTS

This book would not be possible if it were not for those who came before me. My military instructors from basic training to the most advanced officer level schools I had the privilege of attending. My soldiers who I never stopped learning from and the many Non Commissioned Officers who showed me the way (believe what you want but the NCO's do run the Army).

The Army is where I developed my drive to learn more about how and why we act the way we do under high levels of stress in the lethal environment. How is it that a group of people can receive the same training, practice and develop skills to the same standard, and then perform so differently when put to the true test? Well, anyone looking for answers to these questions need only experience the tremendous learning environment created by the likes of Massad Ayoob, Bill Rogers, Ray Chapman, John Farnam, Ken Murray, Dr. James Williams, Michael E. Conti, Martin Michelman, and way too many more to list here.

I have had the privilege of attending the training of most of these men and the others have greatly influenced me through their lectures, seminars or panel discussions. Others shared their expertise through publications of their real life experiences, tactical concepts and research findings. To a man, I could never thank them enough for what I have learned and how that knowledge has influenced my life choices. I hope this book in some small way will continue to enforce the extremely high standards of training and accountability they all so magnificently have established.

Two additional gentlemen that I must take the time to recognize are Dr. Robert Sorensen, and Dr. Edward Godnig. Rob, I know personally as he happens to be a local shooter, friend, and my personal Optometrist. He has a passion for shooting and shooters alike. He has put in countless hours in an effort to help me better understand the low-light issues we discuss throughout this book. His diagrams will provide you with a clear illustration of the facts and a deeper understanding of the low-light world we work in.

As for Dr. Ed Godnig, I have never met this man, but as an industry we all owe him a tremendous debt of gratitude. He has set the standard for Behavioral Optometry which is a clinical discipline that diagnoses and treats visual skills and abilities that have an impact on learning and movement behaviors. Dr. Godnig has a particular interest in enhancing the ability of shooters to use their visual system to improve marksmanship. He has developed visual training exercises for shooters to improve the skills necessary for fast and accurate shooting. He also acts as a consultant to law enforcement professionals specializing in the areas of visual perception and visual attention.

He has graciously given me permission to share the results of his clinical research throughout this book. Because of Dr. Godnig's passion and drive to find the answers and his unselfish willingness to share his knowledge, we are able to understand the darkness in ways that allow us to *Rule the Night*. Take it from me; do not miss the opportunity to read his clinical research study titled, <u>Vision and Shooting</u>.

I hope you enjoy the photography contained in this book. To my very close friend and hunting buddy, Frank Martin of Frank

---

Martin Photography, thank you for your patience, vision and your ability to create art. Another huge thank you to the folks at SureFire, Streamlight, eGear, and First-Light. They really stepped up and offered me the use of their awesome photo galleries. The ability to include such dynamic images has greatly enhanced the look of this book and its message.

Thank You…..

"If your only tool is a hammer then soon every problem will look like a nail"

Massad Ayoob

Why Me?   Why This Book?

For years I have watched armed professionals, military, law enforcement, and private security operators work from a position of self imposed disadvantage while performing their duties in reduced light conditions.   I have often analyzed this behavior in an effort to better understand why this phenomenon is so common among operators of all experience levels. After all, increased anxiety or a high state of stress is nothing new to anyone who has worked as an armed professional.

Why is it though, that we seem to overcome most of these stress related situations when we are working in a lighted environment but continue to falter in low-light situations?   Remember when you completed your Field Training program and worked a patrol shift for the first time in single-man status? I do. I know the anxiety I felt that first swing shift faded away as I became more confident and more comfortable in my new role. As an Army officer, I frequently witnessed a reduced level of duty performance in my soldiers during even moderately stressful operations at night.   Many of these soldiers demonstrated a reduced level of duty performance when put in high stress situations, but eventually learned to overcome their shortfalls. These same duty performance related improvements are much slower to materialize when witnessed under low-light or no-light conditions.   The psychological impact of operating in darkness has a much greater effect on our tactical performance than the physiological limitations encountered.

Over time I have come to believe reduced job performance, or an obvious rise in anxiety among many of these armed professionals has to do more with their lack of confidence in their ability to *Rule the Night*, than anything else. *Rule the Night*, that's ultimately what I am talking about. How can we control our environment and our suspect (threat) through the advantageous use of light? Effective low-light tactics can only be accomplished through cutting-edge training and tactics utilizing top quality equipment.

Through the years we have all been taught dark shadows are potential danger areas. During our career, if we are lucky, we may have a firearms instructor who at least knows the names of a couple of flashlight techniques. But how proficient are they in the coordinated deployment of a light source and firearm? How aggressive were our respective agencies in promoting or even mandating low-light training. Many departments only require a low-light familiarization once a year. It has been my experience that many of these familiarizations were conducted on the firing line without the benefit of any prior classroom or low-light theory instruction.

No wonder a large number of operators lack the confidence to *Rule the Night*. That is the reason for this book. I offer this book as a practical foundation for anyone who has the need or desire to learn low-light tactics. This book is not intended to replace a structured training program, as I believe there is no substitution for instructor/student interaction. The practical application of the necessary theories, skills and philosophies combined with the immediate feedback and critique of student performance by qualified instructors is the ultimate learning experience.

This book is the result of my fascination with how darkness affects our performance. I do not profess to have all the answers. With the passage of every day, my desire to learn more, experiment more, challenge the accepted, and create the new, continues to fuel my fire. The concepts discussed in this book work. Are they all perfect or even suitable for everyone? No, they are not.

Read this book with an open mind. Take the time to try and understand the principles discussed within these pages. You will not immediately perfect many of the skills presented here, nor do I expect you to accept or add all of them to your tactical tool box. More than likely, you will pick a few techniques that work for your style, practice them, modify them as needed, perfect them and I hope by all means use and share them. If you can't perfect a few of these techniques, then they are just not important enough to you to take the time to learn or you are just lazy.

Finally, I have resisted the urge to include Night Vision Systems, Exotic Fighting Equipment and other battlefield innovations in this book. Night Vision Devices and related equipment offer many advantages to those who have access to them. There are many great sources available to you to increase your understanding and improve your skills in these areas. In Chapter 12, I will discuss Laser aiming devices and self illuminating (night) sights as well as alternative light systems and accessories.

My emphasis here is to do the greatest good for the greatest number of operators. The fact is, we all deploy flashlight systems on a daily basis and many do so without a solid foundation in effective theory and techniques. I hope this book will fill the void of information and spark a desire in you to want to learn more. If that happens, then we will all be better at *Ruling the Night and Winning the Fight...*

Be Safe.....

Author's Notes Regarding Book Composition

Gender Consideration – Throughout this book I have used the masculine references he, his, him. This has been done solely to simplify the text and make the reading easier. I trust every female that reads this book will understand I mean no disrespect in this and will not feel excluded from the material content in any way.

"My sole objective in life is to win. There is no room for excuses. Nothing in life is achieved without serious effort. There is no easy road to learning. I will make every effort to keep silent. I will increase my determination to achieve. My training is to correct my own mind."

- The Master's Creed, by Grandmaster Anthony Kemmerlin

The reality of the world we live and work in is becoming more apparent to everyone from the tactically minded to the everyday citizens we serve and protect. Even people who live in rural communities are learning what urbanites have long understood. The night can hold more than mystery, it can be a dangerous environment to work and play in.   Nationally organized community events such as *Take Back the Night* have grown in popularity across the country and seem to reflect the current attitudes of society.   Most people have the ability to pick and choose when and where they work and play. However, tactical operators, law enforcement, and paid security don't have such a luxury. The very nature of what they do requires they spend a great deal of time working in the dark.

The fact is most officer-related shootings occur in low-light situations.   I remember reading FBI data for law enforcement officers killed in the line-of-duty which stated that between 1995 and 2004 over 65% of the deaths occurred between 2000 and 0800 hours. Working in a low-light environment raises the bar for everyone. The need for established tactics and procedures, practice, coordinated communications, and teamwork is even more critical when operations are conducted in low-light conditions.   The simplest movements of a two-man room clearing team become more complicated as we introduce a light source into the darkened environment. We need to see into the shadows. We need to see travel routes and any obstacles that we might encounter. The need to identify friend or foe, threat or non-threat, are all critical elements that must be accomplished without highlighting our position, further degrading our ability to see, or back lighting ourselves or our partners. We must learn to control our suspects and our environment with light. We must establish and maintain the tactical advantage at all times.

What is the "Tactical Advantage"? Ask 10 people and get 10 different answers. In my way of thinking it is a position or operational process that affords you and your fellow operators the best possible opportunity to win the fight. It is moving with the best possible use of available cover.   It is never compromising yourself or fellow team members as a result of poor tactics, techniques or equipment. It is maintaining the initiative of your goal while constantly gathering, processing, and evaluating situational changes. And let us not forget, that true tactical advantage can only be realized and or maintained through good effective communication between you and your team or backup / support personnel.

Operating in the dark or in the low-light environment certainly compounds all of the elements that impact our ability to establish, maintain and expand the tactical advantage.

How do we overcome the darkness? That's what this book is all about. Before we can consider ourselves low-light operators or even attempt to improve our low-light field performance, we must understand how light and darkness affects our eyes. We need to separate fact from myth. We must develop a greater awareness of the equipment available to us and gain the knowledge to make the appropriate equipment selections to satisfy our personal and professional requirements. We must not only see into the night with greater clarity, we must look within ourselves and dedicate some time and energy to learn the skills and tactics necessary to *Rule the Night.*

In addition, we should make every effort to pass this knowledge to those who are beginning their journey. As you become more comfortable with the theories and tactics introduced in this book and develop your own, you will begin to *Rule the Night* rather than just exist in it.

Help yourself and the others who work along side you by sharing your knowledge and experience. We will all be better off because of your efforts. After all, if we are the *Rulers* of the night, that makes the suspects we encounter, our *Servants*.

Operators using the tools…   *Courtesy of SureFire*

What happens to our eyes when we operate in a darkened environment? Why does the lack of light or our inability to see and orient ourselves impact our balance, judgement, motor skills, and our decision making processes? I am sure many of you have never thought of how the lack of light affects how we physically function.   But, I'll bet many of you have experienced both psychological and physiological changes that affect your performance without making the connection to how the lack of light contributed to what you experienced.

In the <u>Vision List Digest</u>: Article 1, Volume 8, Issue 26, Dick Young states "humans are indeed visual". He estimates 80% of the brain's neurons are involved in visual processing. Sensory integration is the process of taking in information from the environment through various sensory systems (touch, smell, sight, movement, sound and the pull of gravity on the body). Information is processed through the brain. The brain then interprets, organizes and directs the body to respond appropriately to that sensory information. According to the Sensory Institute, sensory integration is critical to our overall performance. They state that "if the sensory input is not processed and organized accurately, the result is abnormal motor output with abnormal feedback". I think one of the easiest ways to experience challenges to your sensory input is to subject yourself to the darkness. I seem to learn from every one of these experiences regardless if on the street or in the training environment. If you do nothing else, incorporate low-light shooting into more of your routine range time. If you only have access to outdoor ranges, make the effort to spend a few nighttime hours at the range. If your range has nighttime shooting limitations, you can still learn a great deal from walking through the sequences without actually pulling the trigger.

What follows in this chapter is an overview of the basic anatomy and physiology of how the eye responds to light. I will try my best to keep the material presented in this chapter at a level pertinent to our mission. I believe you must have at least an elementary understanding of how our eyes function in order to appreciate the dynamic effects we experience when we mix darkness, stress, and our eyes. We are indeed visual creatures, so let's learn to take every advantage available as we *Rule the Night.*

The amount and intensity of light entering the eye dictates what neurological information sent via the optic nerve to the brain. Our vision function is divided into three levels of light intensity: daylight (photopic); dusk (mesopic); and low-light night (scotopic).

Photopic – Daylight condition which allows for our best vision. It is under this high level of light that we are capable of 20/20 vision. When light diminishes, the cone function is suppressed and the quality of the eye focusing ability declines. It should come as no surprise that our ability to follow a moving target (called pursuit eye movements) is optimized during photopic viewing conditions. Vision performance or eye movements used when attempting to isolate targets (i.e. target assessment/multiple threat determination known as saccadic eye movements) function much better during bright light conditions than during low light conditions.

Mesopic – Dusk condition drastically reduces our visual efficiency. As we begin this transition our vision is approximately 20/400. Often called the eye adjustment period this is the time we switch from cone dominated vision to rod dominated vision. However, during mesopic vision, both rods and cones are partially active. During mesopia there is a gradual loss of color perception, gradual loss of discerning target detail, and a gradual loss of the ability to maintain accurate eye focus. From a practical standpoint, mesopia is complete when color perception is eliminated, and at this point, the visual system begins to function in scotopia.

Scotopic – Low-light condition, also known as half-moon light, is where we see the greatest drop in operator performance. Personnel operating in this dark environment are legally blind. Vision is typically in the 20/800 range upon initial exposure. Is it any wonder that many police officers killed in low-light situations are killed within 2 minutes of arriving on scene? Your ability to maintain accurate eye focus during scotopic vision is greatly reduced. During this condition you will experience an increased awareness of peripheral light and movement, increased pupil size resulting in less depth of field, and a reduction of contrast sensitivity. When you change from day vision to darkness immediately (e.g. entering a darkened movie theater from the well lit lobby), the dark adaptation of cones is complete in about four to five minutes, while full rod adaptation takes about 30 to 40 minutes. After about 30-40 minutes most people will obtain a visual acuity of approximately 20/200.

Our eyes….Rods and Cones

THE HUMAN EYE - The primary components of the eye that control day vision and night vision are found in the retina and are called the rods and the cones. The retina translates light energy, absorbed by the rods and cones, into nerve impulses to be carried to the brain by the optic nerve. The brain then converts the nerve impulses into images.

CONES - The primary factor in both color vision and detail interpretation during daytime vision is the cones. During the day, the eye tends to rotate to center the image nearer to the area of the retina where the cones are most concentrated. The center three degrees of the retina is made up entirely of cones. This area is called the Fovea.

RODS - The rods are very sensitive to low light levels and determine our ability to see in the dark. At night, our eyes transition from cone dominated vision to rod dominated vision. The result is, we are unable to determine color and determining image detail becomes much more difficult. The peripheral area of the retina contains 120 million rods. The rods are primarily responsible for sending visual information to the brain about movement detection, spatial orientation of where targets may be located and generally adapting to the reduced light levels present in the environment. Since only rods can adjust to the low-light levels available at night, the center three degrees of vision covered by the cones become a blind spot in the center of the field of view. The average field of view for the human eye is about 80 degrees vertical by 170 degrees horizontal.

DARK ADAPTATION - Dark adaptation is an earned advantage. An officer who has dark adapted has a huge advantage over a perpetrator who has not sufficiently adapted. During World War II, pilots would sit and play cards in a dark room with only a red light, so that if duty called, they could run out to their planes and already be adapted. They knew about the earned advantage. An officer who has been out at night should have the earned advantage. Turning on the flashlight for a couple of minutes at a time does not turn the advantage.

The chemical pathway in the cones is Rhodopsin to Retinene to Vitamin A. A quick exposure, or very dim light converts the photosensitive Rhodopsin to Retinene. Retinene is an unstable molecule and will quickly convert back to Rhodopsin if the light/electrical impulse stops within approximately 7 minutes of exposure and if there is adequate supply of Oxygen and Glucose. Smokers have about a 1 minute longer delay in the conversion of Retinene back to Rhodopsin and it is theorized that it's because of lower Oxygen levels. However, if there is extended exposure that is greater than 7 minutes, the Retinene quickly converts to Vitamin A. Vitamin A is a relatively stable molecule and it takes a more prolonged period to convert it back to Rhodopsin again, thus a longer period to dark adapt than to light adapt.

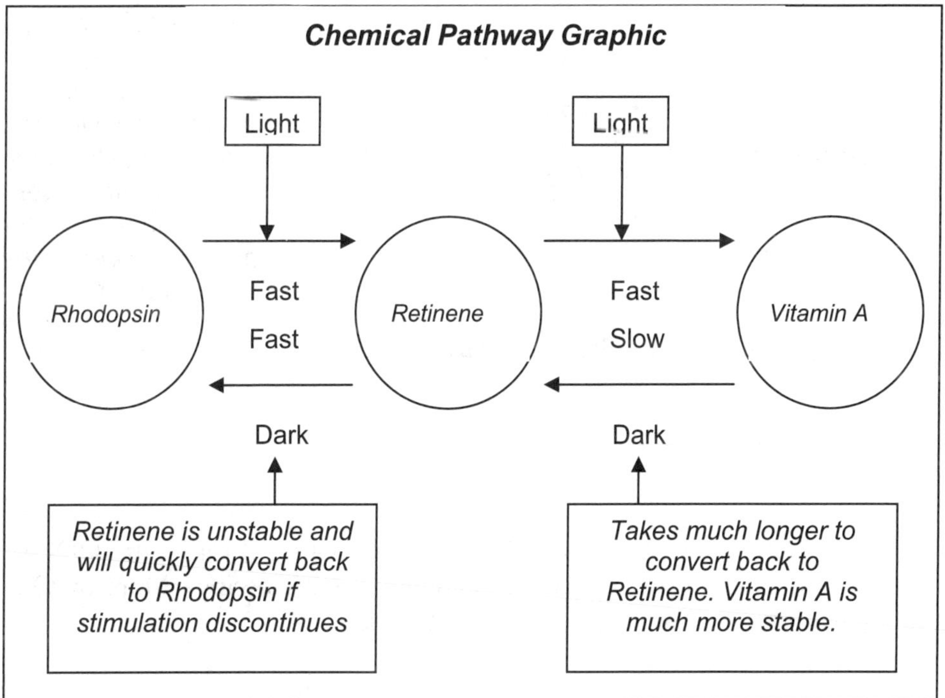

Dr. Robert A. Sorensen told me he sees quite a few pilots in his practice. He teaches them how to see better at night. Particularly, he tells them to divide the night sky into sixteen quadrants. They should search a particular quadrant via eccentric viewing. In other words, in order to search a quadrant they should look into the quadrants around the one that is being observed. This is called eccentric viewing. Macular degeneration patients do it out of necessity. Pilots do it if they want to avoid a crash with another aircraft. Astronomers do it because if you look right at a dim star, there are no cones in that macular region of the eye to detect the light in the scotopic situation.

Look Here	*Look Here*	*Look Here*
Look Here	**Area You Wish To View Detail In**	*Look Here*
Look Here	*Look Here*	*Look Here*

The graphic to the left illustrates Dr. Sorensen's method for eccentric viewing. You will see greater detail in the target area by looking at the area surrounding the target.

Many of us have been doing this eccentric viewing for some time. In our world, it is often referred to as Off Center Viewing. More on Off-Center Viewing in Chapter 5 Visual Patience.

The colors of objects we are trying to identify obviously play a role in our ability to see detail. A person wearing all black will be virtually invisible in the dark. Identifying a blued or dark polymer handgun will be more difficult than the stainless or chrome version. The same can be said about confusing a shiny cell phone with a small stainless handgun. Add movement of the objects we are trying to identify and the process becomes more difficult.

I hope this chapter helped you establish a foundation of knowledge with respect to how our eyes function. It is not inclusive of everything that could be presented on the subject. I have attempted to highlight enough information to support the findings and principles presented throughout this book. Clinical research continues and reports are constantly published. I encourage you to make an effort to stay current with respect to gaining a better understanding of how we see into the night.

"Winning Isn't the Only Thing, the Preparation to Win Is!"

VINCE LOMBARDI

You are the weapon,
anything you use is only a tool.

- SPECIAL FORCES SAYING

Over the years I have observed many students and operators using hand held and weapons mounted lights. As you might expect, most tend to use light in the obvious ways, to navigate, signal, search, communicate, and for identification purposes. Where most miss the boat and put themselves and their partners at an unnecessary disadvantage is they fail to use the light in a CONTROL role. That's right, I believe the most overlooked application for the use of a high intensity, quality light is control. Use the light to control your suspect and your environment. You may be asking yourself, what is this guy talking about? How can I use light as a control tool?

Using light to search and navigate.   Courtesy SureFire

Let's look at how we can take the advantage when using a light in the target identification role. Most use a light to merely locate and identify the target and then take appropriate action. In a building search for instance, you come across the suspect. In the traditional application you light up the suspect and begin taking control of the situation. You more than likely start with verbal controls. You direct the suspect into a position to affect an arrest or at the very least take control to continue your investigation in a safe environment that you feel comfortable in. As you do this, where are you pointing the light? Where are you looking? Most operators are looking at the hands. How many times have we been told to watch the hands? Watch the hands. After all it's the hands that will kill you! What most of you do is you direct the "hot spot" or the brightest part of the light beam where you are looking… at the suspect's hands. Time after time I see this phenomenon repeated over and over again on the street and in my training classes.

Under these circumstances you are working at a compromise. Yes, you are using light in the identification role.   But, think how much safer you would be if you used the light to control the suspect as you are identifying him. All you have to do is direct the hotspot of the light beam into the suspect's eyes. If you keep the light in his eyes, you will have plenty of peripheral light to observe his hands and the suspect will be dominated by your high intensity light in his eyes. Most often, his hands will come to his face in an effort to shield himself from the dominance and discomfort of your light, allowing you to see what if anything he's holding.

Let's just think of the many advantages you realize by applying light as a control tool.   With the light in his eyes he is preoccupied and uncomfortable and will not be able to direct an effective threat your way. He will not be able to look for escape paths or for that matter he will have a very difficult time determining how many of you he is faced with. His discomfort, disorientation, and inability to see clearly in your direction all result in a situation that will be much easier for you to control. The chances are much greater that he will become compliant rather than raise the level of his resistance.

I am not talking about a major change in your tactics. All I am asking you to do is to make a small adjustment in the application of your light/firearm application skills. You will need practice in order to be comfortable in the proper use of the light. Like anything important and worthwhile it will take some effort on your part to get the mechanics down. In addition, you will need to increase your understanding of the human eye as it reacts to light. Your confidence in light as a force option will grow as you increase your understanding of how darkness and light affect the suspect and us emotionally and physically.

These concepts and proof of their effectiveness will be presented throughout this book. The drills and exercises located in the following chapters will assist you in developing the necessary skills you will need to develop techniques, tactics and the mindset that will allow you to *Rule the Night.*

"Those who Hesitate will Meditate Horizontally"

Ed Parker

How do you use light as a force option? I bet I've got you wondering now. Imagine your suspect experiencing 5-7 seconds of disorientation as a result of something you do at your discretion from a distance with your flashlight. Would you do it? Would you flip that preverbal switch just before you go hands on?   I bet you would. I know I do it all the time. It works! One way I often apply this principle is when I am approaching a car on a traffic stop at night. If for some reason I feel the least bit unsure of what I am walking up on, I will flash the driver's mirror with my 150 lumen patrol light. That always results with some choice words from the vehicle occupants. I immediately apologize and explain that I didn't realize I flashed the light in the vehicle's passenger compartment. They typically respond with "no you flashed the mirror and that's where we were all looking". Exactly!

What I accomplished with that light in the mirror was about 7 seconds of disorientation on the driver's part. At the very least, I reduced his ability to see me clearly and mount any type of attack as I approached. I have had drivers who were not even capable of getting their drivers license out of their wallet after experiencing the mirror flash. Try it, you will like the results. Would you find any advantage in putting your suspect in a situation that would take him about 90 seconds to regain approximately 70% of his ability to see that he had before you flashed him with the light? Would you consider that to be a tactical advantage to yourself? Sure you would.

In years past, some officers had their own ideas of alternative uses for their flashlight. To evaluate these applications is not the intent of this chapter. I do feel the need to at least address a couple of them if for no other reason than for their historical significance. Let's look at some of those applications before we get into the force options I want to emphasize in this chapter.

Officers sometimes used the large lights in ways similar to a baton to cause pain compliance through pressure points and various joint locking techniques. Some officers routinely used the larger lights in a modified escort position when moving a handcuffed person.

Another application that immediately comes to mind is using the flashlight as an impact weapon. The size, shape and durability of the larger C and D cell Mag Lights made this application possible. After all, it is a natural progression to transition from using the light in a traditional sense to hitting someone with it when it is already in your hand when the need arises.

Many people say today's "High Neck Index" technique evolved from the position many officers used as they held the large Mag Lights while in the Field Interview (FI) position. Many officers in anticipation of using the light as an impact tool would grasp the light with an ice pick type grip.

He would then rest the butt end of the light high on his shoulder close to the base of his neck. In this position the heavy light was essentially cocked and ready to strike. This is much like the coiling of the bat a hitter in baseball does as he awaits the pitch. Additionally, this positioning of the light helped ease some of the stress and fatigue caused by holding the light away from the body.

Using the light as an impact weapon was not without risk or controversy. Significant injury to the suspect was always a possibility. The civil liability and lack of formalized training were often issues the departments and individual officers faced. After a number of highly publicized injury cases, departments started to restrict the use of the large lights. The Detroit PD removed the large lights from service over 10 years ago. This trend continues across the country today fueled in large part by the proliferation of the small LED lights.

SureFireE2D at left is one example of the smaller LED flashlights available today. Notice the Crenellated Strike Bezel and Scalloped tail cap that could prove valuable if the light was used as an impact weapon.

Photo Courtesy SureFire

A first hand experience that I will long remember with high intensity light as a force option came when I was a student in the SureFire low-light instructor course. My instructor, Bill Murphy dropped me to my knees during the live fire range exercise through the effective application of the SureFire Devastator 500 lumen light. Bill was very close to me when he illuminated my face with this very overpowering light. Not only was the light so intense that it completely shut me down but the heat I felt from the 500 lumen element added to my disorientation. It took me a long time that evening to recover to the point that I could continue shooting. This type of light in the hands of an experienced operator is an awesome force option tool.

If you have a quality light source, and you know how to use it, you can gain the advantages as stated above every time you confront a suspect in a diminished light environment. I can't stress enough that in order to see results as stated above, you must have training, quality equipment, and the confidence to apply the techniques presented in this book. If you are to have a reasonable expectation of the suspect's disorientation, you must know the light flashed in his eyes is free of any dark spots or imperfections. Make sure the light you select and use will project a clean beam/pattern free of any dark spots. Many instructors say you must have a light with a minimum of 65 lumens. I prefer a minimum of 80 lumens. See a complete description of lumens and candle power in Chapter 7 (Equipment Options).

To many people, using light as a force option is a new dynamic. I can't remember ever seeing "The Use of Light" in any of the footnotes that accompany the various Use of Force continuum charts I have looked at. Whether the concept is new to you or not, it deserves your consideration.

Look at both the offensive and defensive applications of quality light as you begin to assess the feasibility of adding light as a force option to your tactical toolbox. We already have enough going against us as we often find ourselves in a reactive mode. How many times have you been told "Action is faster than Reaction"? We all know it to be true.

Typically we utilize tactics, training, and troops to overcome many of the situations we are faced with. Look at the effective deployment of a quality light as another tool to help us win. We are often working in a diminished light environment when we are confronted with a lethal encounter. The very fact that we are in less than desirable lighting conditions means we more than likely are using some type of artificial light.   But, as stated earlier, most of us are only using the light in a traditional sense. In other words, to navigate, investigate, or perhaps communicate.

I tell my civilian students all the time that what makes the "key chain mini-baton" so effective as a defensive weapon is the fact that they have it in their hand when they are most likely to need it, (i.e. opening the car door, office door or house door). So let's look again at the previous paragraph. There you are in a low light environment with the flash light in your hand and you need to take some defensive or offensive action as a result of the suspect's actions. Does it not stand to reason that if you can gain the advantage (either defensive or offensive) by deploying the tool you already have in your hand, you should do it?

The advantages of such actions are many and go way beyond reaction time in its purest sense.   When you consider the reduction in motor skill performance and the time wasted as you decide what tool you are going to deploy after you do something with the light that is already in your hand, the advantages are apparent.   After all we will extend both our reaction time and our movement time if we choose to deploy a tool other than what we already have in our hand.

Don't miss understand me, I am all about getting rid of anything that will not be of benefit to us during those critical situations. This is one of the cornerstones of my motivation to write this book. At a minimum, the coordinated, efficient deployment of a quality flashlight is a tremendous equalizer. In fact, personally I have always felt the light has given me a distinct advantage over my suspect.

In the next chapter titled Visual Patience we will further discuss the Body Alarm Response (BAR) showing further reason for limiting fine motor skill actions whenever possible.

*"If I had six hours to chop down
a tree, I'd spend the first four
sharpening the AXE".*

Abraham Lincoln

Visual patience is a term that comes up in many of my defensive firearm courses. Emotions of the fight and visual patience are often mixed or confused when we attempt to analyze the high stress environment of a gun fight. I often see a lack of visual patience during live fire low-light drills or when we are conducting low-light force on force training scenarios. On the live fire course, I will often expose the student to multiple "bad guy" targets that look identical. Typically these are full color realistic silhouette targets of bad guys holding weapons of some sort. I often raise the intensity of the live fire drills by introducing 3 dimensional mannequin like targets. Many times these mannequins are dressed in clothing (both male & female) to add a sense of realism. What I will often do is replace the weapon on one of the targets with surrender hands. This is a subtle change in the overall appearance of the bad guy. The students will typically fail to take the necessary time to make the appropriate target identification. They fail to have the Visual Patience to properly ID the target as a surrender target and they wind up shooting a target that should have been treated as a no-shoot.

We need to understand that in reduced light, our mind will try to fill in what our eyes can't see. This becomes even more difficult to manage under stressful conditions. Have you ever been hunting and took a break around midday? Perhaps you are sitting on a ridge overlooking the beautiful country side and you see what looks like a bull elk or big mule deer across the way. In your excitement, you pick up your binoculars for a closer look only to find that what you are looking at is a big rock or tree stump.   Well, after you have your lunch and perhaps a short nap you again look over the country side hoping to see that monster bull. Again, in the same spot you see the most majestic animal. Again you get a better look with your binoculars, and again it is that very same rock or tree stump. You see, your mind wants to see that next trophy on your living room wall. As you scan the countryside your mind starts to fill in the blanks. That is when we need visual patience.

Dr. Rob Sorensen tells me he has patients who are missing part of their vision and their brain will actually wallpaper in what it thinks should be there such as the elk that is actually not there. It is not a hallucination, but rather a sort of overlay.

Another aspect of visual patience is the ability to realize that you are utilizing the light correctly. Remember, your effective control of the suspect and your environment depends on the proper use of quality light and tactics such as light beam/firearm bore alignment and displacement.

We have all heard instructors talk about Fight or Flight Response. Lately we are hearing the term Body Alarm Reaction (BAR) in the place of Flight or Flight. The BAR is the body's response to the high stress of a life threatening attack situation. Add the psychological & physiological changes that are magnified by the lack of light and the Low-Light BAR can be the most severe a person will ever experience. The most immediate visual change in response to the BAR is that the eye loses it ability to maintain clear focus on targets at close distances. During the first few seconds that you experience the BAR you are unable to focus on the front sight of a gun. Your visual focus will be drawn to infinity. This is sometimes referred to as getting "Big Eyes". This focusing change toward infinity focus is due to the transition from parasympathetic nervous system control to sympathetic nervous system control.

This shift in the autonomic nervous system balance is responsible for changing how the crystalline lens inside the eye changes its shape and optical power. During the immediate stages of the BAR, the lens becomes less convex in shape and this forces an optical shift of clear focus only while viewing distant targets. The autonomic nervous system has two major branches; the sympathetic and parasympathetic branches. Generally speaking, the sympathetic nervous system prepares the body for direct action and confrontation by increasing heart pulse rate and bringing blood supply to large muscle groups. The pupils dilate just like the aperture in a camera opening up to allow more light in. Opening the aperture lets in more light, which is desirable, however, just like in a camera, opening the aperture can create a whole new set of problems. If the pupil/aperture is wide open, the light rays are coming in at different angles than they would if the aperture were a pinhole.

Remember the pinhole camera that you made out of a shoe box when you were a kid? It was in perfect focus because you eliminated all but the light rays that were coming in perfectly straight. Opening up the pinhole/aperture creates aberration because although there is more light, it's no longer coming straight in. If the pupil is dilated as it is when the sympathetic nervous system is stressed, light isn't coming straight in.

The photoceptors in the eye have directional sensitivity (Stiles-Crawford effect). In other words, they are more sensitive to light coming straight in (small pupil/aperture) than to light coming in scattered. The eye pupil diameter increases, and the ciliary muscle relaxes, forcing a shooter to focus the eyes at far distances, perhaps to be behaviorally better prepared for a perceived oncoming threat.   Some believe there is a slight bulging of the eyes associated with sympathetic nervous system dominance. However, this response may actually be the lids opening wider giving a bulging appearance.

The parasympathetic nervous system allows you to maintain a more relaxed, balanced state of readiness by slowing an accelerated heart rate, which decreases pupil size, and allows the eyes to focus at distances as close as inches from your eyes. The parasympathetic nervous system aims to bring neural physiology back to a state of balance.

When the BAR is activated, along with the neural changes, there are hormonal and other biochemical changes activated concurrently by a part of the brain called the hypothalamus. These chemical mediators are useful in helping maintain the influence of the autonomic nervous system response by either encouraging the body to stay in 'high alert' or by reversing this high intensity response to strong stimuli and resume a more normal relaxed controlled state of neural balance. However, during the early stages of the BAR, adrenalin is released in the body to further enhance the excitatory component of the BAR.

It is important to remember that the sympathetic nervous system can exert its neural messengers either in a focal manner at local end organs (as is the case at the muscle of the eye's focusing system), or through releasing noradrenalin or norepinephrine directly into the bloodstream to prepare the body for combat.

During the BAR there is a series of other biochemical and hormonal changes that are activated throughout the body. Cortisol is a common hormone that increases blood sugar levels to contribute energy for muscle function. Research has also correlated decreased learning and decreased memory function, as well as attention anomalies with increased cortisol levels in the body. These changes in response to cortisol levels increasing during the BAR help explain, in part, why visual memory and visual attention are narrowed during the BAR.

"Tunnel Vision" or "Perceptual Narrowing" can be explained by these physiological changes that accompany the BAR. As humans we have an innate tendency to narrow attention upon a threat during extreme stress. I am constantly teaching my students to train under stressful situations. We have to work at maintaining a broad scope of attention.

Don't fear the light. So many times we hear firearm instructors say "the suspect will shoot at the light so turn it off". Have you ever had an instructor yell "get that light off"? I understand and in fact teach the intermittent use of light. However, don't be so quick to turn off the light that you fail to accomplish the goal you had in mind when you turned it on. I have witnessed my students turn the light on and then quickly shut it off when they take the shots, ultimately shooting a darkened target that they did not have the visual patience to properly identify or assess. Granted, you must have light discipline but, your techniques must allow you the time to realize the tactical advantage and intelligence the light offers.

For obvious reasons visual patience is a skill we all must master. It's been my experience that this is more easily accomplished as your confidence in low-light conditions increases. I see many students succumbing to the increased anxiety of the low-light environment and for some reason think turning the light off and pulling the trigger will get them out and safe sooner rather than later. How often have you heard "you can't shoot fast enough to make up for misses"? Well in the same vain, you can't casually ID a target and recover from shooting a no-shoot.

Dr. A. M. Skeffington, a leader in the study of behavioral optometry, theorized that during high levels of stress, our ability to center on a task and identify and maintain accurate target awareness is severely hampered. BAR type of stress reduces our ability to interpret what we are seeing and establish a visual memory image due to a perceptual narrowing that accompanies the breakdown of optimal human performance. His theory postulated in the 1940s has gained strength and understanding during the last half century as more current neurological and psychological research has proven the bulk of his intuitive understanding of human responses to stress.

Other behavioral and performance changes have been reported to be associated with "perceptual narrowing". The theory of perceptual narrowing suggests that as the level of demand increases on a central, straight ahead target, there will be a corresponding decrease in the visual area surrounding the central area from which peripheral information can be extracted. Increased arousal causes increased narrowing of your focus, with a progressive elimination of input from the more peripheral aspects of the visual field. Another way of viewing "tunnel vision" is that as stress increases, there is a reduction of cues used to regulate performance. When stress levels are further increased, there is a further restriction in the range of visual cues used to sample visual space. Under stress, the useful field of view shrinks and the amount of processing of visual information is narrowed.

A summary of behavioral changes that are associated with high levels of stress as seen during the BAR, include;

- Narrowing of attention span and range of perceived alternatives,
- Reduction in problem-solving capabilities,
- Oversight of long-term consequences,
- Inefficiency in information search strategies,
- Difficulties in maintaining attention to fine detail
- Temporary loss of fine visual-motor coordination with intense fear.

As I have stated earlier, much of the clinical information presented here is the result of Dr. Ed Godnig's research. He indicates, during the active stages of the BAR, it may be difficult to recall with high accuracy and detail the events that just occurred during a life and death shooting exchange. However, after the high stress is relieved and the shooter returns to a more normal or relaxed state, they may recall more of the events as they occurred.

Visual information travels from the retina to the brain by way of a dual pathway system. One pathway (M-pathway) is more sensitive to course visual forms and quick moving images. The (P-pathway) is more sensitive to fine spatial details of forms that are slow moving or stationary.

Under high stress there seems to be an imbalance between the P and M pathways to the point that one pathway overrides the other. "Tunnel vision" appears to be related to the P-pathway dominance and the M-pathway inhibition during the BAR.

Target contrast and the colors of objects are critical variables that relate to the ease of visibility or recognition. Contrast corresponds to the ability to discriminate a dark image from a light image. Colors have a direct influence on visibility in a daylight environment. It has no influence in low-light conditions.

The following is Dr. Godnig's list of visual skills that are important to a shooter's speed and ability to aim accurately.

- **Visual acuity:** Both static (discerning detail of a stationary target) and dynamic visual acuity (discerning detail of a moving target) is important to a marksman. Good dynamic acuity will enhance a shooter's visual reaction time and eye tracking abilities.

- **Peripheral vision:** Skillful shooters have reported a visual ability of maintaining an awareness of a central target while simultaneously maintaining a vast amount of peripheral visual awareness. A fully functioning visual system is capable of responding to objects located within a total visual field (which for each eye is approximately 40 degrees up, 60 degrees toward the nose, 70 degrees down and 90 degrees towards the temple measured from the central point of fixation). It is critical that shooters are aware of what is beyond and around the target to insure safety, and peripheral vision awareness is crucial to achieve this task.

- **Depth perception:** An essential skill for the shooter who needs to judge relative distances between targets.

- **Eye motility:** Eye tracking abilities are crucial to maintain accurate detail and awareness of any moving target. This skill is highly critical if a marksman needs to shoot a moving target.

- **Eye-hand-body-mind coordination:** A necessary set of visual coordinated abilities that are used in developing precise trigger control while maintaining precise aim on target.

- **Visualization:** The ability to use your "minds eye" to create a mental visual picture when direct view of a target may not be possible. This highly developed visual skill is useful to anticipate where a target or adversary is most likely to be located during episodes of lack of direct vision.

- **Speed of recognition time:** Extremely important when a target may be only visible for a brief moment in time. The ability to accurately recognize as much of a target in as little as 0.01 seconds can be critical in deciding to shoot, or not shoot a target.

- **Eye focusing flexibility:** This ability plays an extremely important part of a shooter's ability to quickly adjust focus upon targets that are located in different distances in space. The speed and flexibility of quickly changing eye focus from one point in space to another point in space has a direct influence on maintaining clear, single binocular vision while in a shooting competition or in combat.

- **Color perception:** May prove to be a useful skill when confronted with the need to engage targets of specific coloring.

- **Fixation ability:** Necessary to establish "sight picture" awareness and consistency.

- **Visual memory:** Used to embed the learning elements of training to help skills reach the point of automaticity. Training to the point of automaticity implies that the speed of processing and performing a set of skills is fast, there is a relative lack of effort to perform a skill, and that skill is autonomous such that it may be initiated and run completely on its own without active voluntary conscious thought process. The automaticity realization of shooting skills is useful in avoiding visual perceptual overload resulting in confusion in target recognition.

- **Central-peripheral awareness:** The ability to have awareness of central details of a target and simultaneously be aware of the visual space surrounding the target (the peripheral space around the target). This skill helps a shooter avoid getting locked into "tunnel vision" for extended periods of time.

Most of the skills listed above (except for color vision) have a learned component involved in the acquisition of the skill. Not only can you train to improve these skills but there are tests available to determine how well you are doing. Sports visual training is the optometric art and science of fine tuning and enhancing your visual skills and abilities.

You should take the time to work with a sports vision specialist. A 1995 research report discussed a three month visual training program conducted with the Catalan Government Special Intervention Squad at the Olympic Training Center in Spain. Pre-test and post-test results were compared for pistol shooting performance and visual function. Statistical analysis revealed significant gains in visual function and pistol shooting scores after the training program.

"Unless you do your best, the day will come when, tired and hungry, you will halt just short of the goal you were ordered to reach, and by halting you will make useless the efforts and deaths of thousands."

- Gen. George S. Patton

Anyone who has studied or even read about tactics has heard of Colonel Boyd's OODA Loop. Serious students of tactics have taken the time to appreciate the simplicity and effectiveness of Boyd's OODA Loop theory. They are better operators as a result of their OODA Loop understanding. Before we discuss the concept, and how we can apply its principles to the low-light fight, let's look at its origin.

USAF, Col John Boyd coined the term and developed the concept of the "OODA Loop" (Observe, Orient, Decide, Act) originally called the "Boyd Cycle".   During the 1950s John Boyd dominated fighter aviation in the U.S. Air Force.   He built his notoriety flying the F-100 aircraft. Boyd was often referred to as "Forty-Second Boyd" because he had a standing challenge to all pilots that if they could defeat him in a simulated dogfight in less than 40 seconds he would pay them $40.   It is said that Boyd routinely accepted challenges to his 40 second simulation, but he was never defeated.

Boyd was famous for a maneuver he called "flat-plating the bird." In the defensive position with a challenger in close pursuit Boyd would aggressively pull the stick back to its physical limit and apply full rudder.   His aircraft would flip 90 degrees and rapidly reduce speed from 400 to 150 knots in seconds.   The enemy pilot who was once the hunter immediately became the hunted.

Many people credit Boyd's OODA Loop as changing the air war in Korea. Boyd simply realized that United States pilots were flying aircraft that could not outrun their enemy. He was able to take advantage of the unmatched maneuverability of the U.S. planes and give the pilots tactics to defeat their enemy. In more recent time Boyd was called in to consult with our war planners during Operation Desert Storm. In fact, Secretary of Defense Dick Cheney has credited Boyd's influence as a major reason he changed the battle plan for the liberation of Kuwait from a frontal assault, which could have led to many American casualties, to the "left hook" that proved so successful.

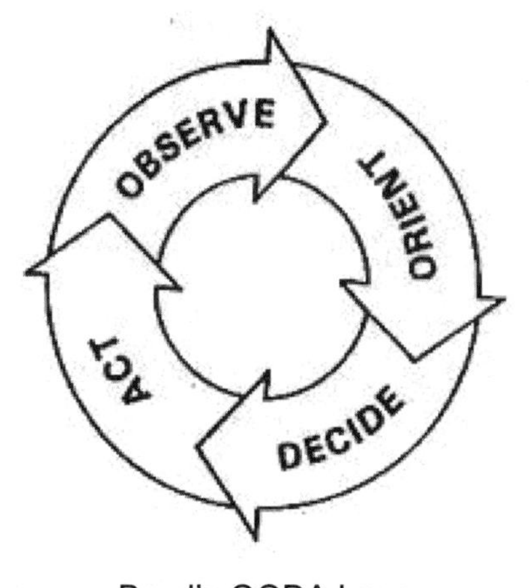

Boyd's OODA Loop

For our purposes, Boyd's OODA loop illustrates the steps we must go through before deciding on a course of action. Staying in your OODA Loop and causing your opponent to restart his will yield you the advantage every time. Typically, you stay in your OODA Loop cycle through movement and dynamic action. Your movement will at the very least, allow you to take the initiative of the fight.

I believe, if you can stay in your OODA Loop and cause your opponent to restart his, you will win. Easier said than done? Not really. Let's take a look at how to bring this technique from the Korean War to the urban battlefield many of us face on a daily basis. Your primary goal should be to stay in your OODA Loop.

I am not asking you to do anything you don't already do on a daily basis. For example, when behind the wheel of your car you come to the intersection of a roadway and the parking lot you are attempting to exit. You OBSERVE the oncoming traffic. Then you ORIENT yourself to the traffic and DECIDE the course of ACTION. What is your action? Do you hold the brake allowing the traffic to pass, or do you depress the gas peddle and move into the flow of traffic?

That is as pure an example of the OODA Loop cycle that I can describe. The good news is that it really doesn't get much more difficult when applied in a combat or tactical situation. Recently I was dispatched to transport a gentleman who was being violated by his probation officer. This subject had stated many times that he was never going back to jail. As I walked down the hall towards the probation officer's office, the suspect saw me approaching and made the correct assumption that his time as a free man was rapidly coming to an end.

He jumped out of his chair, bladed himself towards me and balled up his fists. This action immediately started the OODA Loop cycle for us both. Realizing this fact, I refused to start my OODA Loop cycle over. I stayed in my initial cycle which forced the subject to restart his again and by then I had the advantage and he went to jail without further consequence.

How did I do this? Easy, as I approached him and saw that he was standing and preparing for a fight, using a command voice, I simply called out his name and directed him to stand up. This really confused him because it was clear that he was already standing. It also caused him to start his OODA Loop all over again. He was standing there with this dumb look on his face trying to figure out what I was talking about. This allowed me to stay with my original OODA Loop cycle which gave me the time to get to him, go hands on and take him into custody without incident.

In this state of confusion he started his OODA Loop cycle each time I did something different. Once with my verbal command, then as I went hands on, then during the hookup, and again during the pat down, etc... Properly using the OODA Loop will give you the advantage. What really made this happen was the fact that I had a preplanned response in mind if faced with resistance. My intent was to direct him to stand. The fact that he stood up as soon as he saw me did not change my preplanned response. Who knows what may have happened had I not had a preplanned course of action. The delay alone in my reaction to his action (as I would have had to develop a response) would have put me at a distinct disadvantage.

How might this work in a gunfight? Well, let's assume you come face to face with a gunman. At the moment you both see each other you each start your OODA Loop cycle. If neither person does anything to force the other out of theirs, the winner will be the fastest gun, or the best shot, or who knows. I don't know about you, but I want better odds than that.

In the scenario above if you make an aggressive move off the line of attack, you will cause your opponent to start his cycle all over again. Every time you take the initiative you will force a delay (however small) in your opponent's response. This will improve your odds and give you an advantage. If nothing else, it will be harder for your subject to hit a moving target.

"A good warrior knows how to use many tools, but a great warrior knows when to abort them and go to something else".

-Tony Blauer

Previously in this book I made the following statement *"Effective Low-Light tactics can only be accomplished through cutting-edge training and tactics utilizing top quality equipment"*.

What is top quality equipment? That is a question my staff and I are asked on a daily basis. The answer is not as easy as you may think. Lights come from so many manufacturers offered in so many varieties, styles and price ranges. You have hand-held, weapons mounted, vehicle mounted and now even a lighting system that you wear. Regardless of the style chosen, a primary point of evaluation must be the quality of the light beam. After all, the tactical advantages that we discuss throughout this book can only be realized with a quality beam of light. In this chapter we will discuss the specific criteria that I feel must be met in the selection process of a true tactical flashlight.

Chapter 8 is where you will be introduced to the many techniques and principles of deploying the light in an advantageous manner to your situation and environment. I am convinced that you must use the light source in coordination with the firearm and other tools to make a complete lethal system. Coordinated utilization of the light and firearm will allow you to gain and maintain the tactical advantage. Make no mistake about it, the improper use of light can be hazardous to yourself and those around you. More about that in the chapters to come.

Like everything else flashlights have continued to improve with technology. They are brighter, lighter, and packed with features we would never have considered possible just 10 years ago. Remember that commercial catch phrase from many years ago? *"You've come a long way baby"*. I don't think anyone would argue that this is especially true of the tactical flashlight market.

Manufacturers like SureFire and Streamlight have paved the way with innovation, quality and technology. In the early years, police officers used generic flashlights, as conventional thinking of the time was you only use a light to see into the night. I wonder what the locker room conversation would have sounded like had someone talked about controlling a suspect merely with the use of the light beam and not the flashlight barrel. Fact is the

---

light beam quality available in the early years was barely adequate for navigation let alone any offensive or defensive application. In the mid to late sixties many cops carried an aluminum bodied, D-cell Kel-light named after its inventor Don Keller. Given the Kel-light's size and weight many officers carried it as an alternative impact weapon more that they did for light.

In the 70's and 80's the law enforcement community started to see the rechargeable light gain in popularity. Streamlight and Mag Light led the way with a number of models. Many of the lights of this era were large and heavy. In the early 80's the LAPD was looking for a smaller bodied light that could be weapons mounted. In anticipation of the many roles they were sure to be challenged with during the 1984 Olympics they contacted Dr. John Matthews president of Laser Products. Dr. Matthews developed a weapons mounted light powered by lithium batteries. The lithium battery powered technology soon allowed for smaller handheld lights. In the late 80's Laser Products introduced the SureFire 6P. Due to its size and performance, the 6P changed the way police officers used flashlights forever.

As a community I believe we must pay homage to the likes of Don Keller, Dr. John Matthews, Ken Good, and many other pioneers who were determined to reinvent the light and looked beyond the traditional applications of light.

Whether it is hand-held, weapons mounted or even if you wear it, to be considered a "true performer" the light must meet some specific criteria. Let's take a look at what I believe are essential elements of any duty light.

<u>Reliability</u>

It should come as no surprise that reliability is a critical aspect of any light you put in your toolbox. After all, have we not always been told the number one criteria of any handgun used for defense is *functional reliability?*   Many of you will find the light application techniques that you will soon be introduced to foreign to your previous understanding. As you begin to rely on your newly found application techniques and start to truly *Rule the Night* you will see the offensive and defensive value of your chosen light.   You must have a light that works how and when you expect it to. Never compromise on reliability in an attempt to save a few dollars.

<u>Beam Quality & Brightness</u>

Technology has evolved and we are the ones who have benefited. The lights are smaller, lighter, and brighter. They're not cheap but as more and more manufacturers and suppliers enter the market the costs seem to be stabilizing some.

Arguably the greatest benefit of a competitive market has been in the quality of the light beam. Light Emitting Diode (LED) technology is changing daily. In the last 3 years I have been collaborating with a company called eGear, Inc. to produce the ultimate line of extreme use tactical lights. During this time I have been so excited over a new LED version only to see it trumped by the next latest and greatest. As an industry, we are now reaping the benefits of the Cree LED. It would not surprise me in the least if by the time you read this book the Cree will be old news.

The beam needs to be bright and free of imperfections. Imperfections such as dark spots or rings compromise the effectiveness of the light. Most beams have what I call the hot spot. The hot spot is the bright center portion of the beam. There are many ways to measure the quality of light output. In the past Candlepower was a popular way of assessing a measurable value to the light. However, for our purposes candlepower is not a true measure of light quality. Candlepower is the measure of the light at the source. We are more concerned about the value/intensity of the light as it is projected. In other words, the measure of total light output called Lumens. Lumens are a much more accurate measure of light for the tactical environment.

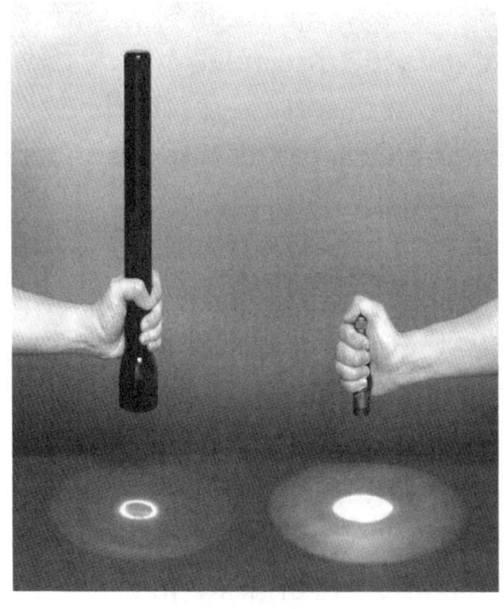

The illustration on the left clearly shows the tremendous capability of the smaller lights.

The beam produced by the light on the right is brighter, void of imperfections or dark spots, and well suited for our purposes.

Photo courtesy of SureFire

I believe 80 Lumens is the minimum intensity necessary for our purposes. All things being equal, I will always opt for the highest Lumen value. With high Lumen output comes shorter burn times as the power draw on the batteries is greater. Unfortunately it's a compromise between Lumen output and burn time.

Reflector design and innovation has played an extremely important role in the development of high-end lights. I am a big fan of the pre-focused beam lights. Designers have been able to maximize the performance of their lights because the innovations in reflector design have kept pace with LED technology.

Before leaving our discussion on beam performance, let's discuss the element of beam whiteness. The "white light" of the modern LED's is a much cleaner looking light as compared to the traditional filament bulb. Like most things in our world, you don't get something for nothing. What this bright white light costs us is penetration through smoke. Throw a flash-bang in a room and enter with only white LED light and you will notice a significant reduction in penetration. Your ability to see deep into the corners of the room will be less than you are accustomed to with the traditional bulb. Keep this in mind as you evaluate the mission and develop your tactical plan. At the very least, you should be aware of the light choices of your team members. Many teams mix and match their light sources so they are never completely relying on any one system or technology. Some team members will deploy LED lights and others will deploy incandescent bulb technology.

Strobe Function

A number of companies are offering tactical lights with a strobe function.   In 2004 Blackhawk introduced the Gladius a multifunction handheld light with a strobe feature. This light was designed and developed by retired Navy SEAL Ken Good.

I really like the strobe feature in a tactical light. At the very least it is very annoying if you are on the receiving end. I find the strobe drastically reduces my suspect's ability to track my movements as I maneuver throughout the scene.   In a non-clinical assessment, I can say without hesitation, my students hate the strobe feature when I use it against them during force on force training.   Many indicate an increased feeling of disorientation or confusion. The bright flashing light seems to force the subject to alter their OODA Loop and in some cases brings on a feeling of nausea. Many feel the best application of the strobe is when used in conjunction with a constant beam provided by another officer. This dual application of flashing and constant light affords you and your team the best possible elements of visibility for you and disorientation on the part of the suspect.   Experiment and try different deployment techniques to determine what works for you.

I have tried a number of strobe lights and it should come as no surprise that the higher output lights with the fastest strobe feature seem to be the most effective. Don't overlook the potential benefits of a strobe feature as you begin your search for the perfect light for your circumstances.

Power Options

Your evaluation of appropriate light systems must encompass their power systems. The advances in power sources have made many of the current flashlight innovations possible. Evaluate the battery types, C, D, AA, Alkaline, Lithium, Ni-Cd, rechargeable, battery packs and just about any other combination you can think of.   Each power source has unique characteristics you need to consider. Cost however, is the one most often asked about by my students and customers.

The illustration on the left is an example of battery evolution in our tactical lights.

As the power sources became more powerful and smaller, so did the lights.

Alkaline batteries have long been the favorite power sources in many applications. They have a lower initial cost and offer a steadily declining power output. If you were to graph the output of the Alkaline power source it would resemble a triangle or ramp. The new battery with full power would show a constant decline until the battery was out of power.

Compare that to the new Lithium battery and the graph would have a steady output for some time and then drop off quickly. A disadvantage here is you don't get much warning that you are about to be out of power. The Lithium batteries have a shelf life of over 10 years and provide very good performance in cold weather environments. They are one of the most powerful batteries for its size. Of course the size/power output does not come without a higher price tag. Recently we have seen the prices of Lithium batteries become much more affordable.

Ni-Cd batteries offer great power capabilities but they self discharge over time. There are many variations of both Ni-Cd batteries and their chargers. The discharge rate of the Ni-Cd is constant and unlike the Lithium batteries, Ni-Cd users have more warning of power outage. Systems that offer both AC/DC charging features allow you to charge your light in the vehicle as well as on your kitchen counter. Some chargers allow you to charge the battery pack without the flashlight. This allows you to use the light while the spare battery pack is charging.

WHICH LIGHT? – Just like your firearm choice, try to select the light based on your intended application. In many cases this may necessitate the selection of more than one light. For instance, I believe while on duty, every officer should have at least one pocket or pocket clip size light on their person in addition to the patrol light they wear on their duty belt. You should consider a light similar to the Surefire E2D, the eGear S-2 or the eGear PDL-2. These small but very powerful lights are very unobtrusive and are more than capable of getting you out of a jam if you suddenly find yourself without a light. The output of these lights range from 60 to 100 lumens with outstanding beam quality. Some special features include a removable spring steel pocket clip, a tail cap momentary push button with a rotate for lock "on" operation and is O-ring sealed.

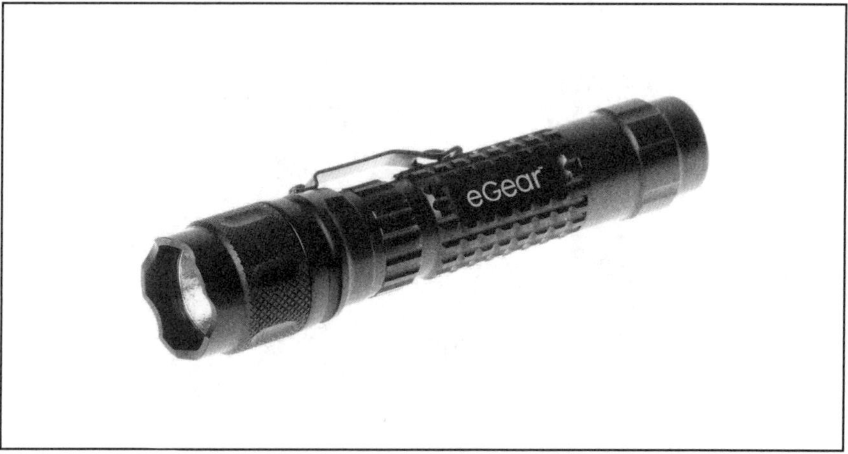

Above eGear's PDL-2 an 80 Lumen mini belt clip light

Below eGear's S-2 an 80 lumen light powered by AA batteries

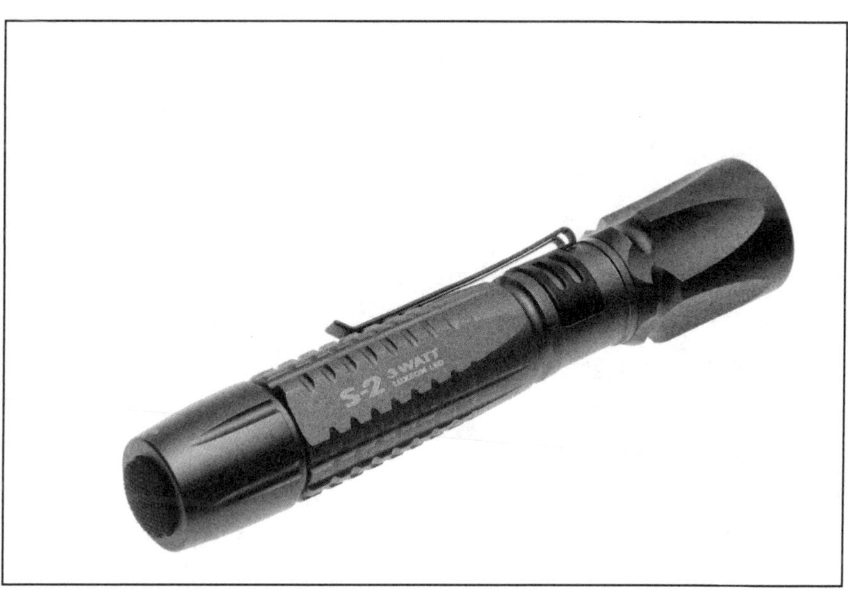

Above Streamlight's Stinger TL-3   Courtesy Streamlight

PATROL LIGHT CONSIDERATIONS – The Streamlight TL-3 LED model uses a Luxeon, super-high flux LED that is 10 times brighter than a generic high-intensity LED thus giving you the longevity of an LED with the brightness of a high-powered conventional bulb. The output is 85 Lumens. It uses the three 3 volt lithium (10 year shelf life) and a Luxeon, 5 watt Bulb, super high-flux, 10,000-hour LED. The light is made of machined aircraft aluminum with anodized finish and high-temperature glass lens. This light weighs 198 grams with batteries. It boasts a runtime of 4 hours of high brightness and 50 hours of declining brightness.

Some special features include removable spring steel pocket clip with adjustable wrist lanyard, an adjustable spot-to-flood focus, tail cap momentary push button with a rotate for lock "on" and is O-ring sealed.

eGear's new tactical light the TAKEDOWN™

Another workhorse that is available at a very competitive price is eGear's latest addition to their xtreme tactical light family the "Takedown™". The eGear company built this light based on my specifications. The name comes from the first thing that popped into my mind when I tested the prototype for the first time. It was at night when I switched the light on and it immediately reminded me of the blinding takedown lights on my patrol car light bar. The Takedown is a 150 lumen light sized to be worn on the duty belt utilizing Cree LED technology. This light has two output levels and a strobe feature. The strobe cycles at approximately seven flashes per second. It is a rechargeable light that will soon set the standard in patrol duty lights.

The Takedown has a lifetime warranty and is affordably priced for the law enforcement market. What impresses me the most about this light is the quality of the light beam. It is bright, clear of imperfections and has piercing quality to it.

SureFire has a number of great patrol sized lights in their inventory. From the G3 Nitrolon® to the KROMA®. The G3-BK Compact high-intensity incandescent flashlight for tactical, self-defense, and general use, similar to their very popular G2 but a slightly longer, more powerful three-battery version. The G3 puts out a smooth, brilliant, pre-focused tactical-level beam with five times the light of a big two D-cell flashlight—bright enough to temporarily blind and disorient an attacker by impairing his night-adapted vision.

The KROMA® is a compact (pocket sized), high-intensity, selectable output/multi-spectrum LED flashlight for tactical, self-defense, recreational, and general use. The Kroma's virtually indestructible primary light emitting diode (LED) provides two output levels of white light. They include a long-running low beam and a brilliant tactical-level high beam with nearly three times the light of a larger two D-cell flashlight—enough light to temporarily

SureFire Kroma

blind an assailant. Its TIR (total internal reflection) lens ensures that the primary beam is perfectly focused—no dark holes, hot spots, or shadows.

Red and blue secondary LEDs also feature two output levels suitable for operations requiring minimal light for preserving night vision while navigating, tracking, map reading, or other close work or for negotiating outdoor terrain without disturbing wildlife (many animals can't see red light). A rotating selector ring allows for no-look control with just a twist to change beam color or output level.

The Stinger DS™ LED is the first dual switch light I have ever used. The folks at Streamlight say "two switches are better than one"! The Stinger DS™ LED is the only rechargeable flashlight with a fully independent dual switch. This light is easy to use. You can access any of the three variable lighting modes and strobe via the tail cap or the head-mounted switch which operates independently from the tail cap switch.

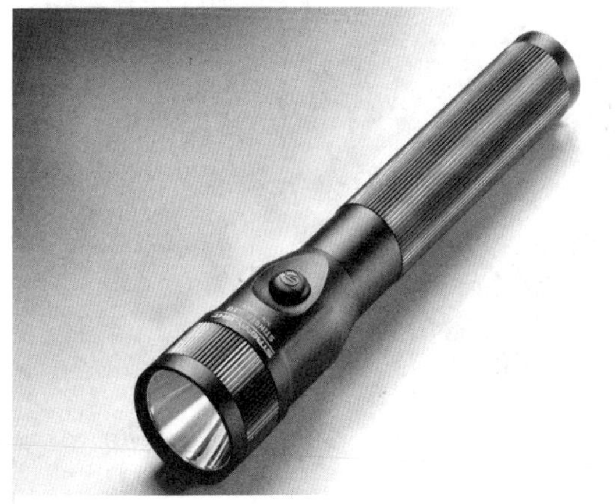

Streamlight Stinger DS™   Courtesy: Streamlight

A deep-dish design parabolic reflector produces a long range targeting beam with optimal illumination to aid in navigation. The output is rated at 80 Lumens and includes a switch to strobe feature. Streamlight indicates runtimes ranging from 1.75 to 6.75 depending on the power setting.   I like the size and fit of this light. It is just under 9" long and is well balanced and weighs 12.8 oz.

The light is made from 6000 series machined aircraft aluminum with non-slip rubberized comfort grip and sports an unbreakable Polycarbonate lens with scratch-resistant coating. It has O-Ring sealed construction and a 3 watt super high flux LED, impervious to shock. It is powered by a 3-cell, 3.6 Volt Nickel cadmium sub-C battery that is rechargeable up to 1000 times. The good news is this light fits existing Stinger chargers.

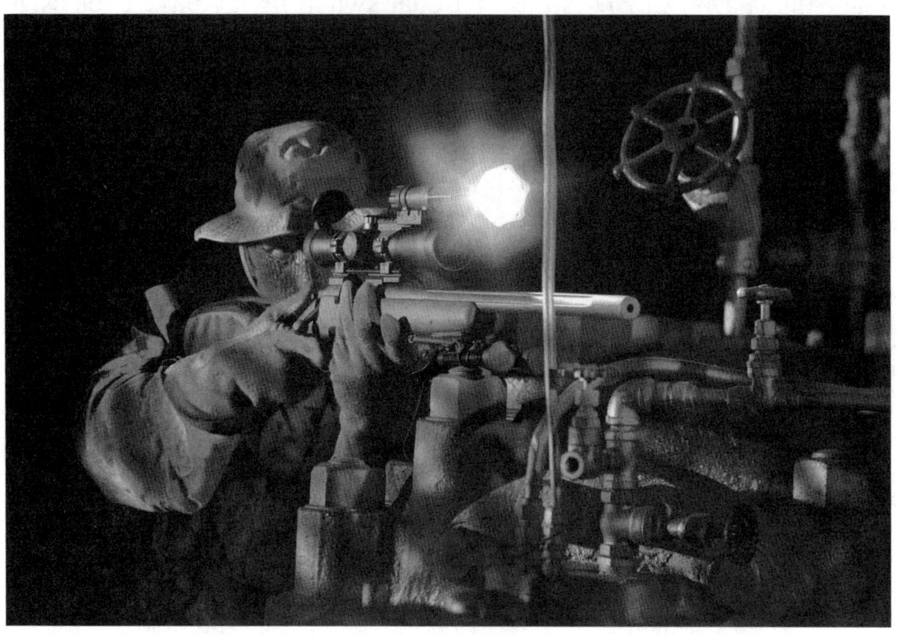

Above: Precision rifleman gaining the advantage.   Courtesy SureFire

WEAPONS MOUNTED CONSIDERATIONS – Like the hand held versions previously discussed, the weapon mounted lights are getting smaller and brighter.   There are many high quality weapons mounted systems for you to choose from based on your budget and mission. Listed below are a few lights that I have used and believe warrant your consideration.

The SureFire X200B® features aluminum body construction and a 5-watt high-output LED surrounded by a micro-textured reflector. While the A model is designed to produce a tighter beam for identification of longer range threats, the wider beam of the B

X200B in use.   Courtesy SureFire

model is better for peripheral threat identification. The window is constructed of tempered Pyrex® and has an anti-reflective coating. The X200B's Rail-Lock™ system clamps solidly to both the Universal Standard rail as well as the MIL STD M-1913 (Picatinny) rail, and includes adapter plates for both. A momentary toggle/push switch allows fail-safe ambidextrous function under fire.

Insight Tech Gear's new SSL-1 is gaining popularity among my students. The 80 Lumen LED light beam is bright and clear of imperfections. LED life is rated at 10,000 hours and the case is made of Type III Anodized Aluminum. It has an ambidextrous constant and momentary rocker switches. This unit is waterproof to 66 feet and weighs only 4 oz. with batteries.

From Streamlight the TLR-1 Gun Weapon Mounted Tactical Light has many features that should peak your interest. It is an intensely bright, very small and durable tactical light that will attach to almost any gun with minimal effort in just seconds.

Streamlight TLR-1   Courtesy Streamlight

It is powered by two 3-volt CR123A lithium batteries with 10-year storage life. It is a shockproof 3-watt Luxeon LED with blinding beam (up to 80 lumens) with bright side-light that will not break or burn out! Run time is up to 2.5 hours. The rail grip clamp system securely attaches/detaches quickly and safely with no tools and without putting your hands in front of the muzzle. This light features fast, adjustable, secure side mounting to 1911 and Glock style Rails. The body is machined aluminum sealed construction with black anodized finish. It is waterproof to one meter for one hour, dustproof and has ambidextrous momentary/steady on-off switch with highly accurate sight repeatability when removing and remounting.

For rifle applications make sure you evaluate the two-battery Scout Light from SureFire pictured on the next page. This system attaches to a Picatinny rail via an included thumbscrew clamp. An extremely rugged and powerful LED module produces 100 lumens of electronically-regulated light with a total runtime of nearly three hours. Switching is accomplished with a momentary-on remote tape switch that can be unplugged from the light if repairs or adjustments are required.   It has a maximum output of 100 lumens for 1 hour, then lower output for over 1.5 hours. Total runtime 2.5+ hours.

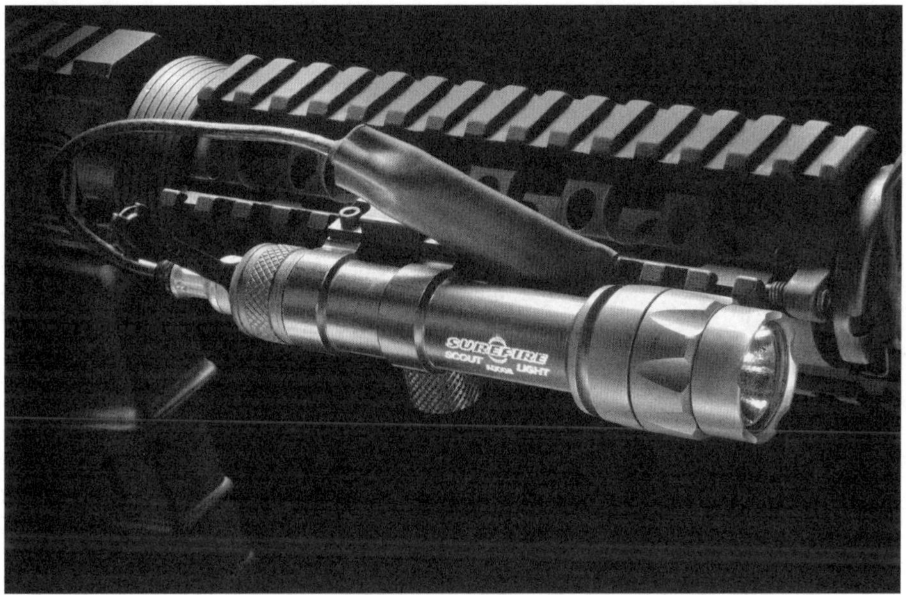

SureFire Scout series light. Courtesy SureFire

There is no shortage of possible solutions for Shotgun use. Everything from clamp mounted to dedicated fore-ends is available.

If a dedicated fore-end appeals to you, take a look at the SureFire system. They offer replacement fore-ends with integral tactical lights to fit many popular shotgun models. These fore-ends come with a pressure sensitive activation pad for momentary light use, and a constant On/Off switch ("F" models only). A P60 lamp assembly is standard, providing 65 lumens of light for one hour. The P61 ultra-high output lamp assembly can also be installed, boosting output to 120 lumens for 20 minutes of runtime. Constant-on and momentary switch are standard and optional system disable switch is also available. This switch is a useful feature for covert operations or to eliminate accidental light activation during storage.

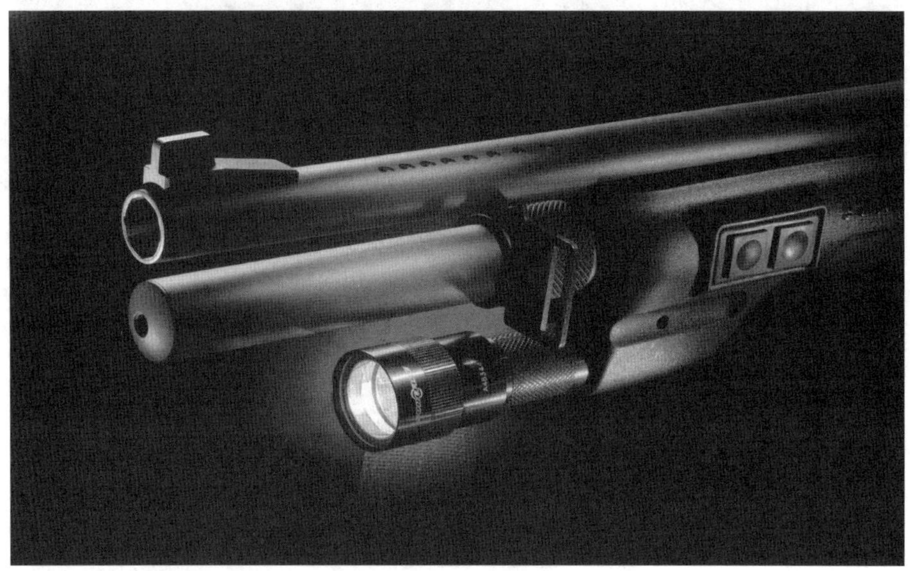

SureFire 618FA System. Courtesy SureFire

SureFire shotgun replacement fore-ends feature a shock-isolated bezel/lamp assembly and a machined barrier between the lamp and battery stick to prevent the battery stick from slamming into the rear of the lamp during recoil. Batteries within the battery stick are separated by a fiber washer and held within a plastic sleeve as further insurance against recoil-related failure.

Throughout this book I have been very careful not to promote any one specific brand, model, or style of equipment. In fact the purpose of this chapter is to provide a broad based list or inventory of the most popular lighting systems in use today. A few weeks ago I thought I had this chapter completed. I felt good about the number of lights covered and the range of manufacturers seemed to include the most common and certainly the most recognized brands in use today. I even mentioned the uniquely designed and deployed "First-light" lighting system.

However, at the 2007 International Law Enforcement Educators & Trainers Association (ILEETA) conference in Chicago, I attended the first ever First-Light Instructor Certification Course. The First-Light system impressed me so much that I delayed the printing of this book so I could modify the First-Light information presented in this Chapter.

Is First-Light for everyone? Probably not. There will be some that will not even give this lighting system a serious look due to its design and appearance. I have to admit, I kind of fell into that category myself. The First-Light folks have taken a unique approach to solving the many issues associated with the simultaneous use of a flashlight and firearm. They have created a lighting system that you wear. Their design and innovative styling allow you to wear the system for long periods without compromising your comfort, mobility or safety. It is amazing how effective and versatile this system can become with just a little practice. The more interaction I had with the First-Light system the more I came to realize my initial coverage in this very chapter came dangerously close to selling the system short. I am very glad I had the opportunity to get up close and personal with this unique system.

The learning curve with this light was minimal. In a very short period of time, this light remained on my support hand without interference during many simple and complex tasks associated in the law enforcement patrol role. I was able to do pat-downs, room searches, cuffing techniques, deploy OC or Taser and of course shoot my handgun or long gun without compromise. I must admit, not only was it not a hindrance, I do believe my safety and that of those around me was enhanced by my wearing this system.

First Light's   Liberator

The Liberator as it is called was developed by First-Light CEO & Founder Jeremy Ross. Jeremy, while negotiating a tree stand in the dark with bow in one hand, flashlight in his mouth, and gear in the other hand, thought there had to be a better way. That led to a wooden prototype, then a PVC version, and ultimately many machined anodized metal prototypes which led to the latest version of the Liberator.

As of this printing, the Liberator by First-Light has models featuring between 80 - 120 Lumen output. Run time varies based on output levels from 90 minutes to 60 hours. Knowing the First-Light gang the way that I do, I can only imagine what innovations are yet to come. The uniqueness of the Liberator goes way beyond its appearance and I recommend you take a serious look at this system. I find myself saying, why didn't I think of this?

Liberator with Weapon System   Courtesy: First-Light

*"There are no extraordinary men…
just extraordinary circumstances that
ordinary men are forced to deal with".*

Admiral William "Bull" Halsey

What technique do you like? What's that called? How do you hold the light? I hate the way I shoot using that grip. My fingers are too long or my fingers are too short, I could never use that system.   Do the previous statements ring a bell? They do for me.   They can be heard in and around the low-light classroom or firing line every time people gather to shoot in the dark.

What is still mind boggling to me is the fact that many firearm instructors don't have a clue when it comes to teaching the skills of manipulating a flashlight and handgun simultaneously. In fact, it has been my experience that many instructors don't even know the names or pros and cons of the most common techniques. We must challenge ourselves to not only be familiar with the techniques but, we must understand the ergonomic limitations/advantages as well as the physiology of the human eye.

I hope I was successful in the previous chapters in establishing a foundation of understanding with regard to the physical and psychological factors of the Body Alarm Response (BAR) and low-light shooting. Now it is time to put into practice techniques and tactics that will allow us to *Rule the Night.* How do we do this? Which is the magical technique that guarantees our survival?

Massad Ayoob in his book <u>StressFire Volume I,</u> states he has been asked, "Why do you and Ray Chapman teach as many as five flashlight techniques in light of the fact that so few cops involved in gunfights use flashlights?" His response is, "The statistics are like that because so few cops are trained to properly use their flashlights. If they were, more would be used in after dark shootouts". Massad Ayoob's assessment is absolutely correct. Instructors and end users must change this phenomenon.

I teach or demonstrate as many as nine different flashlight techniques in my low-light courses. In this chapter we will discuss 6 of the most popular. The techniques presented in this chapter are not all inclusive. They are merely a representation of some of the most commonly used. Do I use them all? Not really. Do I expect you to perfect and apply them all? Absolutely not. Do I expect you to try them all? Yes! Some, you will naturally favor. Others will feel awkward. Pick two or three that make sense to you and put them into your tactical tool box. The more you practice these techniques the more comfortable you will be in their application.

Before we look at the various flashlight deployment techniques let's consider the immediate action scenarios and how to cope with them while operating in the dark with the flashlight and firearm. We said earlier that functional reliability is a critical element of both your firearm and flashlight. However, nothing mechanical works 100 percent of the time. It is during these little hiccups that I speak of here.

You have a firearm malfunction or you run out of ammo. You need to negotiate some type of obstacle that requires at least the use of one hand and it is unsafe to holster your weapon. What do you do with the light? Unless you are using a weapons mounted light system you have to do something with the light.

I have witnessed students putting the lights in their mouth, under their arm pits, in their pockets and even placing them on the floor. I am not a big advocate of placing the light down. I have watched too many students on all fours trying to find it in the dark after they set it down to clear a malfunction.

Obviously the smaller lights that are popular today will allow for easier light and firearm manipulation. Many find the lanyard to be the perfect solution when used in conjunction with these lights. Simply allow the light to dangle from your wrist, complete the task (reload or malfunction clearance) then recover the light and continue your operation.

In the absence of the lanyard, you will have to tuck the light under an armpit, place it between your legs, or between the joints of one of your appendages. I have had a few students who were able to hold their small tactical lights very similar to how one would hold a cigar. Holding the light in this manner they are able to clear type III malfunctions, complete both tactical reloads with retention and of course execute a combat reload. Caution, if the light has been on for some time it may be very hot and could burn you.

Regardless of what you do with the light as you work through the reload or malfunction remember to maintain light discipline. Students will often experience a malfunction during my live fire scenarios. Not sure if it is the stress of the scenario or their desire to do well but, they will often forget light discipline in their efforts to recover from whatever has happened to them. They will go through the entire malfunction clearance with the light on. Not a good move if living is something you wish to continue doing.

What do you do if you are unable to recover from your handgun malfunction? Hopefully transition to your long gun. If the long gun is equipped with a weapons mounted light you are good to go. However, if all you have is your hand held light then some long gun flashlight skills will surely come in handy. There are a number of ways of manipulating the handheld light in conjunction with the long gun.

The flashlight method of switching will greatly influence the technique you use with a specific model long gun. For instance, if you have a tail cap activated light and an AR 15 type rifle you can hold the light in the support hand with syringe grip and grab the magazine well with the support hand (often called the SEAL grip). When you need the light, just squeeze the support hand into the magazine well, the tail cap will depress and the light will activate.

I teach a technique I call the "wobble" to my students. The wobble can be accomplished with any light that has a twist-on switch tail cap. This is the type of switch that you turn clockwise to switch the light on in the constant mode. The wobble can be done with any brand light with this type of tail cap switch. However, it is much easier to do with any of the eGear tactical series lights. That is because eGear has adopted my design of tail cap switch which allows for a greater range of tail cap positioning allowing for the wobble application.

The wobble is accomplished by turning the tail cap until the light is on, then back off until the light just goes off. On some manufacturers lights this positioning of the tail cap is very critical and there is not much of a range to allow the wobble to work. Twist the cap too far and the wobble will not work. Be too close to the constant on and when you apply the wobble the light stays on even without the squeezing pressure. Here is where the eGear light wins as we have designed the threads of the tail cap to allow a much less critical positioning of the tail cap to allow for the wobble.

Back to the application of the wobble technique. Set the tail cap in a position that allows you to switch the light on by squeezing the light barrel or body from the sides. Now place the light in your support hand with the tail cap lying across the base of your little finger. Grasp the fore-end of your long gun with the light positioned between your hand and the forehand. Every time you squeeze your hand around the light and fore-end you will activate the light and its light beam will be in line with the muzzle. Obviously you would probably not do an entry with this technique. However, this method could serve you well as far as getting out of a situation that has gone sideways.

As you begin to evaluate the following techniques take note of how "Hand Confusion" and "Sympathetic Contraction" influence your perception as to what works for you and what doesn't. Hand confusion is a phenomenon many of us have experienced when operating under high levels of stress. It is typically experienced when we attempt to use each hand for separate tasks but somehow it just doesn't work. This is especially true when our hands are in close proximity of each other as in two handed flashlight techniques. For instance you have the light in your support hand while holding your handgun in your dominate hand. You attempt to switch off the firearm safety with your dominate hand and your support hand switches the light on.

Sympathetic contraction can occur at any time but is most often experienced when startled. Many of you are familiar with Dr. Enoka's study on Involuntary Muscular Contractions, 1991. Dr. Enoka is a Professor in the Department of Kinesiology and Applied Physiology at the University of Arizona. According to his study, there are three factors that can cause an officer to experience an unintentional discharge with a handgun. The three conditions include: startle response, balance disturbance and the overflow effect (sympathetic contraction) from the non-shooting hand. If the officer has his handgun out of the holster and the trigger finger is on the trigger when one of these three conditions occurs, the officer's trigger finger can move the trigger to the point the weapon fires without an intent by the officer to discharge the weapon.

Obviously, this same phenomenon holds true for the unintentional switching on of a flashlight. I have witnessed this most often with my students during the initial stages of my force on force training.

HARRIES TECHNIQUE. Developed by Michael Harries, of the old South West Pistol League. This is one of the most common techniques used by my students. I am not sure if its popularity is due to previous training or influenced by Hollywood. Seems like many of the make believe cops we see in the movies or on TV use the Harries.

In the Harries technique, the flashlight is held in the support hand in what is referred to as the "Ice Pick" grip. The goal is to press the backs of both hands together developing isometric tension between the two hands which has a stabilizing effect on the firearm. The elbow of the support hand is pointed towards the ground while the wrist is oriented to align the beam of light with the muzzle direction.   I have witnessed more than one student sweep their support hand with the muzzle while trying to establish the Harries position. Will Long, an FBI firearms instructor showed me a solution he teaches his students (see sequence photos above). Will instructs his students to bring their support hand across their body in the direction of the gun hand elbow while holding the hand and light tight against their upper torso.   This allows you to get the back of the support hand on the opposite side of the gun hand without any chance of muzzle sweep. With the support hand near or under the gun hand elbow, all you need to do is slide the support hand in a downward direction along the extended gun hand, until the back of the hands are together. Since learning this technique I have not seen one student sweep any part of their body.

This is the sequence Will Long taught me for quickly and safely getting into the Harries technique.

Move your support hand as depicted in the photo sequence left – right top - bottom.

Pros:
- Works well with large or small lights
- Works with tail cap and side switch lights
- Two handed shooting technique
- Works well with Weaver Stance

Cons:

- Beam displacement issues
- Light located at shooter's center mass
- Possible muzzle sweeping

ROGERS / SUREFIRE TECHNIQUE. Developed by Bill Rogers a former FBI agent and founder of the Bill Rogers Shooting School. The support hand foundation for Bill's method is sometimes referred to as a syringe grip. Bill positions the barrel of the light between the index and middle fingers of the support hand much like a nurse would hold a syringe while giving you an injection. The tips of at least the ring finger and little finger on the support hand are then wrapped around the gun hand as they would be in a standard two handed shooting grip. Depending on the length of your fingers and the size of the firearm, you may be able to get the tips of all your support hand fingers around the gun hand.

Rogers / SureFire Technique front view

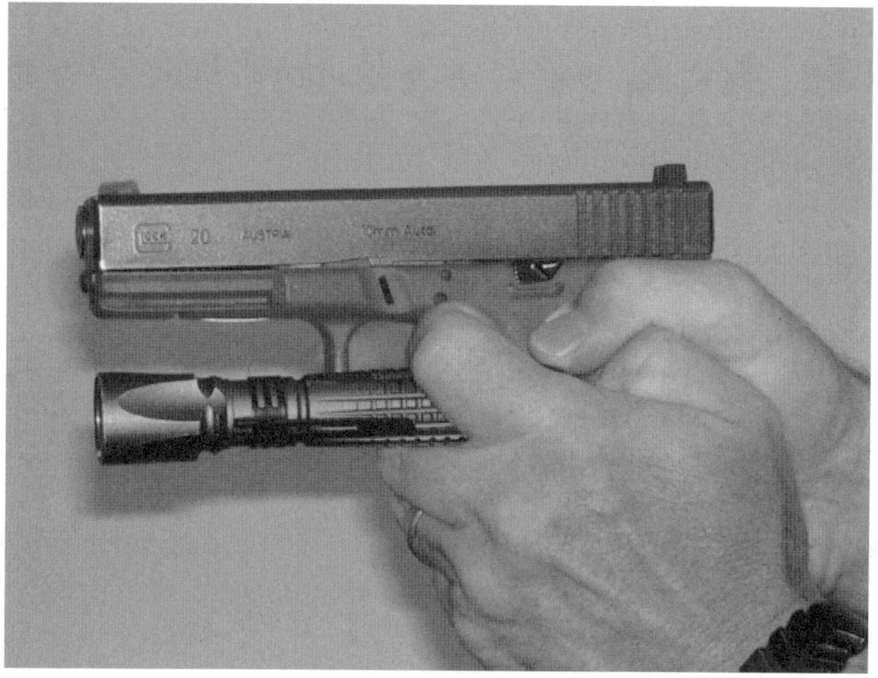

Rogers / SureFire Technique side view

Pros:

- Two handed shooting technique
- Works well with large or small lights
- Natural position when in Weaver Stance

Cons:

- Light located at shooter's center mass
- Beam displacement can be an issue
- Possible muzzle sweeping

MODIFIED FBI TECHNIQUE. (Depicted on next page) Years ago many instructors felt the traditional FBI method was old school.   I believe most of their criticisms centered on the somewhat rigid presentation of both the shooter and the light. Essentially the traditional FBI presentation consisted of the operator holding the light in the support hand while fully extending his arm up and out to the side. Many officers found this method felt very awkward while moving and shooting.

Then came the evolution of the Modified FBI. The modified FBI happens to be one of my favorite techniques. In this version, the rigid almost zombie like movements are replaced by a very dynamic, fluid, and versatile technique.   This is an easy technique to vary the horizontal and vertical presentation of the beam. Transition to other techniques are easily accomplished from the modified FBI.

This technique is very easy to master.   Hold the light in whichever grip you feel most comfortable. The relaxed smooth movement of the light can be best achieved by transitioning the grip or hand position as your overall body position changes. For example, when I have the light high and outside my body I use the Ice-Pick grip. As I transition my arm with the light to a low inside type presentation I often switch to a sword grip. This sounds more complicated that it is. With a little practice the light will always be where you need it without compromising your safety.

The photos on the following page illustrate the many looks and positions of the modern Modified FBI technique. Notice there is no definite, rigid locked in position.

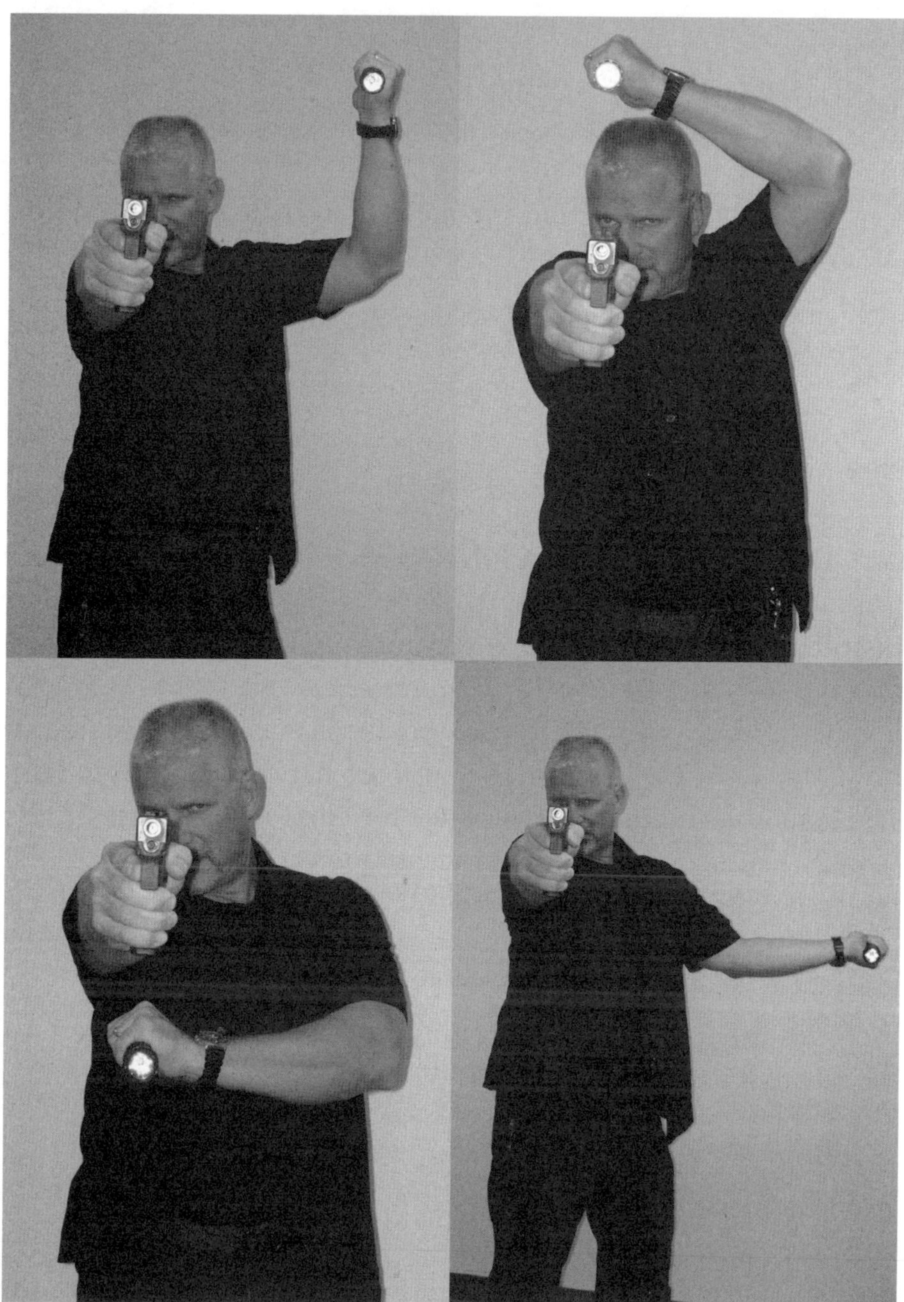

The many positions of the very fluid Modified FBI Technique

Pro:
- Works with large or small lights
- Allows wide range of light movement without muzzle sweep
- Peripheral light from beam can illuminate handgun sights

Cons:
- Limits shooter to one hand shooting
- Practice needed to maintain muzzle and light beam alignment
- Can be fatiguing

AYOOB / CHAPMAN TECHNIQUES. Although two separate techniques in their original forms I have not talked to one other instructor who teaches them separately. I do. In fact, many don't understand the subtle differences between them. I agree in a quick glance they appear to be the same. The difference however, is in the grip of the support hand on the flashlight. The Ayoob technique works better for close in distances of less than 21 feet and the Chapman technique can be used out to the limits of your light beam.

Let's look at the **Ayoob** method. In his book <u>StressFire</u>, Mas indicates this is a close-range anti-personnel technique. He says the key to his technique is "base of thumb meets base of thumb". The natural beam/bore displacement is an advantage here. At close range, when aiming the light beam at the suspects face the gun is leveled at his chest.

The position starts out with the gun in the normal one hand grip position. The support hand is holding the light with a traditional barrel grip. Both hands come together very quickly and point towards the desired location. The theory here is the gun recoils in the direction of the open fingers of the gun hand, the support hand holding the flashlight blocks the recoil and shortens recovery time very effectively. Mas recommends this technique at distances less than seven yards due to the beam angle and firearm bore alignment.

You can alter the beam alignment as you practice this technique to allow for the most advantageous application of the light's hotspot. Practice with this technique will help determine the distance between you and your subject that you feel comfortable.

Above photo shows the front view of the Ayoob technique. Notice the angle of the light beam and the muzzle. The light is clearly in the suspect's eyes and the muzzle pointed at center mass. You can see why Mas teaches this technique for close in distances. Below is a side view of the technique. Notice the alignment of the thumbs.

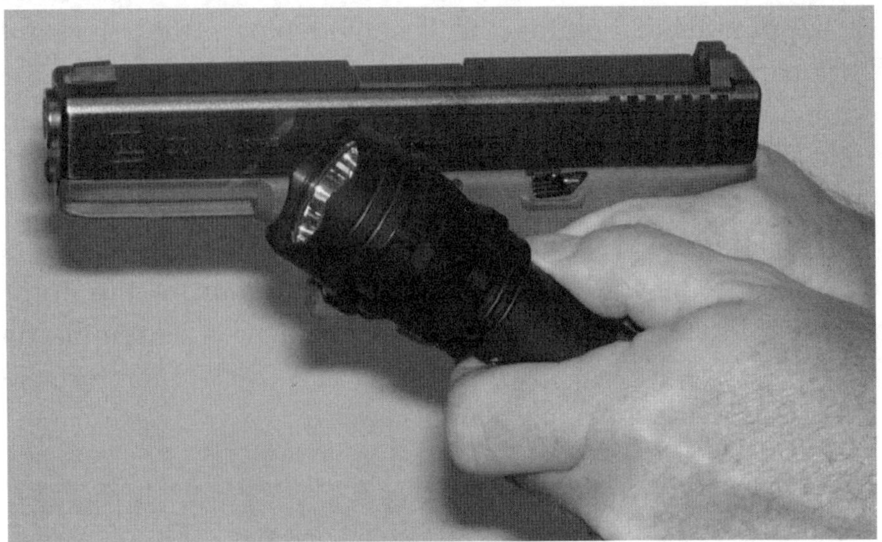

Pros:

- Works with the sword grip
- Light is naturally in suspect's eyes at close distances
- Two handed technique
- Easy transition with firearm from shooting to high ready positions

Cons:

- Limited to side switch lights
- Handgun and light often make contact that results in noise
- Light is located at shooter's center mass

The **Chapman** method was developed by Ray Chapman specifically for winning nighttime combat shoots. To do the Chapman technique, you make an "OK" sign with your support hand by placing the flashlight between the thumb and forefinger. The other three fingers wrap around the gun hand in a more traditional two handed grip. Then align the tube/barrel of the light along your support hand thumb and your light beam should be very closely aligned with the gun barrel.

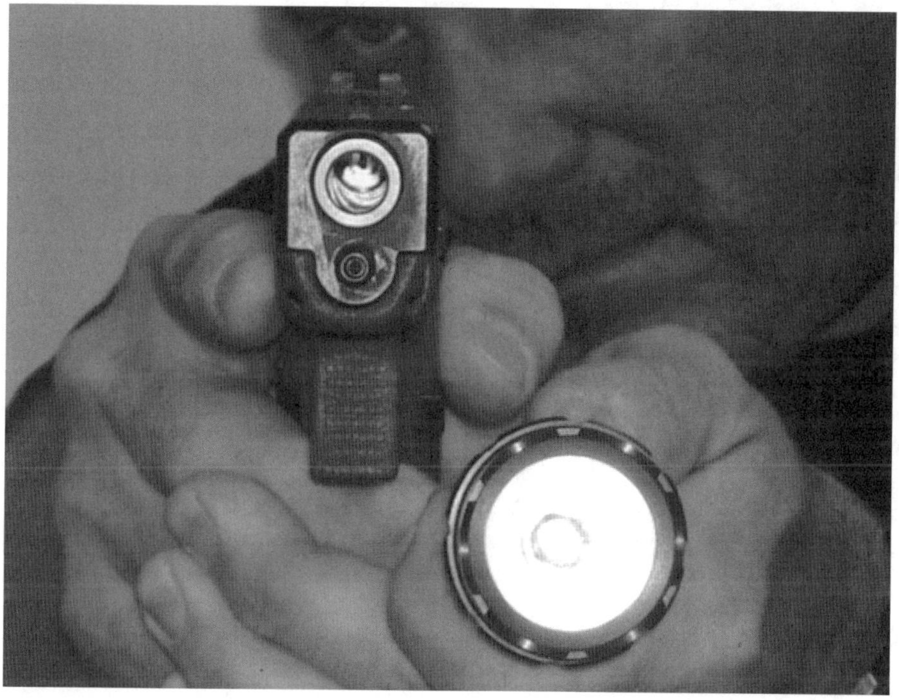

Above is the front view of the Chapman technique. Notice the OK grip made with the thumb and forefinger of the support hand. The support hand bottom fingers wrap around gun hand in a fairly normal grip.

Below is a side view of the Chapman technique.

Pros:

- Works well with large or small flashlights
- Two handed technique
- Very stable position for long range searching

Cons:

- Limited to side switch lights
- Light is located at shooter's center mass
- Fatiguing when used for long periods of time

HIGH NECK INDEX. This is another of my favorites. I first saw this technique demonstrated in a handgun magazine article in the early to mid nineties.

In this technique you maintain a great degree of fluidity in your movement. Transitions from one technique to another are very easy. You can use the peripheral light from the light to illuminate the sights of your firearm.

Start this technique by gripping the light in an Ice-pick grip and bring the light up to your neck. It's important to practice the anchor position required for this method that feels comfortable but will not create a silhouette of your head. I liken this anchor position like an archer would use his jaw to index the same spot every time he draws his bow. Be aware of the position of the light relative to your facial profile. If you get the light too far to the rear the peripheral light will negatively affect your night vision.

Pros:
- Works with large and small lights
- Peripheral light from beam can illuminate handgun sights
- Allows for searching without muzzle sweep

Cons:
- Limits user to one hand shooting
- Can draw fire towards users head
- Can create excess light reflection from back of user's handgun

In my Low-Light courses I teach many flashlight techniques. Do I expect my students to learn them all? Do I expect the students to accept or feel comfortable with all of them? Absolutely not. I hope the students will find two or three techniques that work for them. I hope they will practice them and become proficient in the deployment of these techniques so that they may better keep themselves safe and ultimately *Rule the Night.*

*"One of the biggest reasons for
failure in the field of battle is not
what to do next…this is the result
of not having been trained thoroughly
in what to expect on the battlefield".*

- General Orlando Ward, 1954

Creating the System…You're probably thinking, what is he talking about? Being a firearms instructor and not a literary, "System" is the word that best describes my thoughts here. I don't mean to imply that the effective use of light be a mechanical, rigid technique that can't be modified or altered once initiated. Nothing could be further from my concept of effective dynamic light use. I guess for the purposes of this chapter, if you were to look up the word "System" in the Ed Santos dictionary, the definition would read something like this: System – The deployment of fluid, efficient, proven light use techniques you have practiced and developed a level of tactical proficiency.

Creating a system that works for you is not the easiest thing to do. You have to put in some trigger time to know what works. Students are often frustrated when initially attempting to learn a new technique. This frustration results in a premature assessment of what the technique truly has to offer. I caution you, and recommend you spend some time with any technique that you initially see some value in. Give each technique an evaluation period prior to giving up on it. When you find two or three techniques that work, Practice! Practice! Pactice!

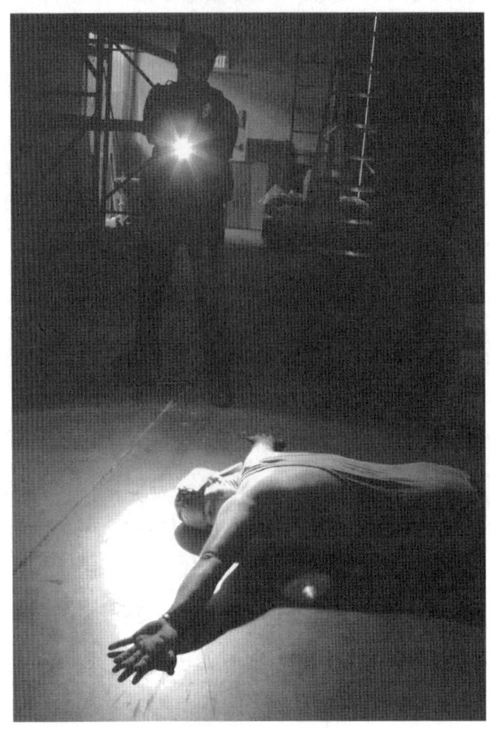

Using the light   Courtesy SureFire

Your practice should include switching from one technique to another technique in every conceivable fashion. Understand the pros and cons of the dynamics of your situation change. The techniques that ultimately make it into your tool box need to be practiced on a regular basis. I would say the more technical or advanced the skill, the more perishable the skill.

Regardless of the techniques you use, knowing when to switch the light on and off is a topic of much discussion among instructors and students. How often have you heard "get that light off", "turn that off", "why did you leave that light on so long"? I agree that light discipline is very important. However, the majority of my students are so concerned about getting the light off that they were not able to identify or evaluate what they were looking at. You must have the visual patience to keep the light on long enough to accomplish your task. I have not been able to find one documented case of a police officer being shot as a result of keeping their light on too long. That being said make it a priority to develop light discipline techniques that will afford you the visibility and the stealth needed to stay safe.

Before we start putting our system together let's consider some basic low-light application principles that you should apply regardless of the technique used. Years ago, when I attended the SureFire Academy, head instructor, Bill Murphy taught us some very effective principles of Low Light Tactics. These principles included the following: Off-Center vision; Read the Light; Operate from the Lowest Level Of Light; Avoid Backlighting; See From The Threats Viewpoint; Dominate With Light; and Light and Move.

Let's look a little more closely at these theories to truly appreciate their value in the low-light environment. "Off-Center Vision". At night, to get the most acute vision you must shift your vision slightly to one side, say 5 to 15 degrees so that the light falls primarily on the rods. The rods on the peripheral of the retina provide our highest resolution vision in a low-light environment. Close to the center of the retina is a small depression known as the yellow spot, or macula. There is a tiny rod-free region at its center, the fovea centralis. Here the cones are thinner and more densely packed than anywhere else in the retina. Since the fovea provides the sharpest and most detailed information, the eyeball is continuously moving, so that light from the object of primary interest falls on this region.

In a dark environment this area becomes a blind spot. To compensate for the blind spot in the center of the field of view, an observer should use off-center vision. This is the Eccentric vision as Dr. Sorensen called it in the earlier chapters. Eccentric or Off-center vision involves looking off to the side of the object of interest then scanning its periphery using short three-second movements. If necessary refer back to Dr. Sorensen's graph in chapter 2 for further clarification. Three seconds allows the rods adequate stimulation time. In the dark, extra stimulation time is needed for the rods to gather sufficient information to form visual images.

I can still hear Bill saying "Read the Light". What he really wanted us to do was evaluate our environment. You must be able to look over the area and make some clear assessments. Are any of you thinking "O" as in OBSERVE in the OODA Loop cycle. That's right. Observe and assess the levels of light, the shadows, the darker areas, cover concealment, movement and anything else that allows you to gain an advantage. After all, your bad guy can only be in the areas that are not illuminated and that you can't see into. Subconsciously at this point you are starting to create a plan.

What are the overall lighting conditions you are "reading"? Are you faced with a blinding light? Is this light so bright that you can't assess what is before you? How about the light behind you? If you move will you become the classic silhouette target? Can you direct enough light forward to overcome the backlight condition? What about the dark holes? Identify what areas you can't see into. How can you get a look into them without compromising yourself or your team? How will the contents of the room affect your use of the light? What in the room could cause you to compromise yourself with your own light? Take the time to make an accurate assessment of your environment. After all, your plan of action will be based on the information processed by this observation.

The whole idea here is to illuminate the bad guy and keep as stealth as possible. Even in the most dynamic entries, you always want to be in a darker less visible position than your suspect. This would be the "Operate from the lowest level of light" principle.   Avoid backlighting yourself or your partner. Ever wonder why most of the paper targets we shoot at the range are dark silhouettes printed on light backgrounds. A silhouetted target is easy to hit and I believe because this image is so ingrained into the shooters mind, you are a much higher risk target when backlit.

Try to look at the overall scene from the suspect's perspective. Try to imagine what he is seeing when he looks in your direction. Where would you hide if you were him? How would you respond to someone approaching from your direction? This goes along with the Visual Patience I talked about earlier. You must take the time to evaluate and appreciate what you are looking at.

My take on Bill's principle of "Dominate with Light" is that of control. I want my students to use light as a control device. I always preach, control your environment as much as possible. You can be very proactive in controlling the suspect and ultimately your environment by effectively using your light to dominate the suspect. Keep the hot spot of the beam in his eye. If available use the strobe feature to confuse and disorientate your suspect. Dave Wittrock, an instructor with First-Light USA, has a technique he calls "Corralling the Suspect". He sweeps the search area with the light. This forces the suspect to continue to move away from the light. With the controlled sweeping and clearing of the light, Dave has directed (or Corralled) the suspect to a known or desired location. If this doesn't fit the definition of control, I don't know what does.

This control aspect of tactical light use is what excites me the most. Don't underestimate its value to your overall safety. The ability to control your environment and your suspect is dependent on equipment and technique. Practice the light and firearm manipulation skills until the light feels like a natural extension to your shooting platform. At that point the controlling process becomes automatic and you will ultimately be safer for your efforts.

"Light and Move.... Move and Light". This sounds so simple but under stress you would not believe how many students fail to do it. In every low-light class I teach I witness students lighting the target then turning off the light and shooting. Or, they shoot the target without regard of the light beam direction. They will turn on the light and move off the line of attack and then turn off the light. Most of this can be corrected by spending more time in low-light training situations under supervision. I say under supervision because many of the students deny doing what I previously described until I play back the video I shot during the exercise.

Keeping with movement and light, the high power lights have a tendency to turn off slowly. What I mean is you switch off the bright light and the light seems to slowly glow gradually down until it is completely off.   If you switch the light off and immediately move, you broadcast your direction of movement. So much for the stealth approach.   What that looks like from the suspect's perspective is the hot bright light slowly trailing off in a particular direction. You can defeat this by waiting for the light to be totally off, or immediately covering the bezel after you switch the light off or by teaching yourself to direct the bezel end away from where you believe the suspect to be.

If you are really on your game you could use this phenomenon to create a little misdirection. If you believe the suspect is able to see your light you can use the light glow to make him believe you went in the opposite direction. You switch the light off, keep it facing the suspect and move the light in the opposite direction you intend to go. When the light is completely out you quietly move in the opposite direction.

These are but a few of the considerations and principles that can greatly improve your ability to *Rule the Night.* I believe in these principles and like many instructors have incorporated them into my overall low-light program.   How you apply these principles, the OODA Loop theory, the newest technology in lights, and your physical attributes and limitations is what makes your system unique. People who have great physical dexterity and fitness may be able to use techniques that other operators could not. Attributes of a particular technique may become even more of an advantage or disadvantage to one operator over another based on their physical ability.

As you begin to put light techniques together and create your system keep an open mind and maintain a realistic view of your capabilities. You may even think of this system as a football coach's game day playbook. You have this broad foundation of practiced skill sets available for you to use. Much like the coach calls plays based on the game situation, you are able to deploy the technique you feel most appropriate to your environment and conditions. Neither you nor the football coach ever expects to use every single option in the book. But knowing the playbook sure makes the ride to the game a little easier.

Think of the light system that you have developed as the "Great Equalizer". At the very least, effective use of quality light tools and techniques will allow you to turn a tactically disadvantaged lighting environment into a positive safer situation. On the other hand, poor low-light skills and ineffective equipment can be a major liability. Poor technique at the very least will telegraph your location and could actually provide a better target for your suspect. Ineffective equipment could hinder your ability to see the suspect, control your environment and even give you a false sense of security.

As I stated in the introduction of this book, I hope you will share your experiences and knowledge with as many of your colleagues as possible. This is especially true with the System you ultimately develop for yourself. Through sharing these techniques you will reinforce your own learning and comprehension to the point that you will become smooth with the skills that will keep you alive. We all know that smoothness leads to speed and proficiency. In addition, through this knowledge sharing you will gain insight and varied opinions of your interpretations as well. Perhaps those you are attempting to help may offer suggestions or questions that when answered, leave you with a better way.

Let us never forget: *"Under extreme stress we will never exceed our level of training. Train the way you will fight as you will fight the way you train".*

Unknown

"I don't care if I fall as long as someone else picks up my gun and keeps on shooting".

\- Ernesto "Che" Guevara

Before we get into how to incorporate the live fire range time into your low-light training program, let's consider a few additional safety measures necessary for low-light live fire. You will need to require all your Range Officers (RO's) to have at least two flashlights on their person at all times. You will want to advise all your RO's and assistant instructors to put filters on their primary light. These filters serve two purposes. First, the filters will allow your staff to better protect/preserve their night vision. Second, it is easier for you to immediately distinguish between a staff member and student from any distance in the range.

Down range activity must be very closely controlled. At the end of any down range activity (grading targets, repairing or resetting targets) I require an RO to walk the entire down range area and report to the Range Master (RM) prior to the commencement of any further training. This may not work for you, but consider some method to verify the down range status. After the RO reports to the RM and prior to the start of the next exercise the RM will twice call out "is anyone down range". Not hearing any response, the RM will then declare the down range area clear.

Student accountability is very critical when working in the dark. Prior to any exercise beginning and after the down range area has been cleared, the RM will have all students count off to verify the presence of all personnel. This count off is required after every movement of personnel down range.

Whenever personnel availability allows, assign one RO the task of observation only. Ask this person to stay disconnected from the student instructor interaction and concentrate on the overall live fire operation. This person has free run of the entire range area and is in constant contact with the RM.

Since visibility is an issue, use additional range commands to maintain a safe firing line.

Some of these commands are listed below:

- Is anyone not holstered?
- Is anyone not loaded?
- Is anyone not UNLOADED?
- Is there anyone who does not understand the course of fire?
- Is anyone not ready?
- Is there anyone who has not completed the exercise?

A few additional items to include in your low-light live fire training pertain specifically to the students themselves. Advise everyone on the range to limit all unnecessary talking unless they are on break. The only talking that should be taking place is that between an individual student and instructor or from a staff member to the entire class.

You should aggressively monitor and require that all firearms remain holstered unless directed otherwise. In addition, require that all student flashlights remain off unless they are directed otherwise. You won't believe how this flashlight rule will impact your overall training. Your students, staff and you will be more rested and everyone will maintain their night vision throughout the night. Your staff and the students will soon come to appreciate the student flashlight discipline.

You may also consider the addition of reflective tape or safety strips to mark personnel or range obstacles or boundaries. I often clip on a small flashing light called the Guardian to the back of the student's hat. These lights can be set to constant on or flash mode by altering the battery polarity. They come in a variety of colors and can be used to identify specific personnel or groups. In summary, with respect to safety, Be alert, Be prepared, Be ready for the unexpected, and don't take any shortcuts.

Now that you are ready for the low-light live fire range, start out with some flashlight drills designed to acclimate the students to the darkness and their lights. One of the first drills you can do is line the students in two rows facing each other with about 3 feet between them. Then have each student pass his light to the student facing him. Now have each row of students take 3 steps back. Typically they will be approximately 20 feet apart. From this distance have one row flash or apply the light into the face of the person directly across from him. The light that is being flashed in the student's eyes is his own, and the reason for the flashlight exchange in the first step.

This empowers the student to realize the efficiency and the power of his own light. This way the student knows without any doubt what the suspect is experiencing when he uses that very light against him.   While the student is experiencing the power of his own light in his eyes, ask him, "Can you see the person flashing the light in your eyes? What kind of detail, if any can you sees? Is he pointing a gun at you? How many people are with him? Can you find cover or a place to run to?" Once this is done have the other row flash the lights they are holding and repeat the entire process.

To further illustrate the dynamic effect the above drill can have, put a student down range about 25 feet away. Then put the hot spot of your light in his eyes. While in this position, control him with verbal commands. At the same time have a student or staff person flank the student and come in behind him and make contact. Then ask the student you are controlling if he had any idea he was being flanked by another officer.   This demonstration is of course done in front of the entire class.

Another tool you can use is the object identification drill. To do this drill you can use a person as a prop or a color lifelike law enforcement paper target. I use the full color lifelike targets for much of my live fire training. The exercise begins with the person or target positioned down range approximately 25 yards away. One by one each student is instructed to illuminate and slowly walk towards the person/target until he can absolutely determine what the object is in the hand of the suspect. The student is instructed to stop the instant he can identify the object and call out what the object is. If he is correct, mark the floor with tape and put his name on it. If he is wrong instruct him to continue closer and repeat the process.

After every student has completed this drill, bring up the lights and as a class evaluate the many different distances represented by the various students' ability to identify the object. This is truly a powerful lesson and illustration of how we all see differently in the dark. It relates back to the issue of visual patience we discussed in the previous chapters. A student that had to get a lot closer to the target in this drill will not be so quick to make a snap judgment as to the identification of an object. I have found they also will be a little more tolerant of a partner who may be having a difficult time identifying an object.

These are but a few of the non-gun related drills I put my students through when we first get to the live fire range. I resist the temptation to do these drills in the classroom as I have come to appreciate the positive effect they have on the students when done on the range. Use this time to observe the students in the dark. Watch for their light handling skills, their low-light confidence, and assess the low-light adaptability of their eyes. You will notice some students moving with confidence and much faster than others. This may very well be an indicator of the speed at which their eyes are adapting to the low-light levels. Use this time to assess your staff and confirm their individual and overall responsibilities as well.

The first flashlight and gun handling techniques are introduced with unloaded firearms. We will do a number of firearm and flashlight manipulation drills to assess everyone's competence level. This is a great time for you and your staff to get to know the abilities of the class.

Start out with the following gun only techniques: draw; acquire the target; return to high ready; 360 degree scan for additional threats; then reluctantly holster. You should be observing to ensure that all the necessary safety and performance standards are being achieved. Now is the time to recognize, identify, and correct any unsafe student. *Indexing throughout the drill to include the holstering process is critical.*

When you feel comfortable with the gun only techniques, introduce the flashlight. The simultaneous manipulation of the light and firearm is when the fun really begins. Practice all the techniques that were presented in the classroom. Refer to them by the correct names and the appropriate safe application techniques are reinforced. As their skills in basic manipulation improve, you should become more critical about light beam and gun bore alignment and of course light discipline in general. The live fire exercises will be much more effective and safer if you can get the students using the light correctly now with the unloaded firearms.

Test their manipulation skills during this cold range period by positioning the targets at various distances. During this time I am constantly reinforcing the visual patience principles discussed earlier and the technical application of the light and firearm as one seamless process. Once you feel everyone is on the same sheet of music, the staff is acclimated, the students are functioning at an acceptable level and everyone has safety as a top priority, then and only then should you instruct them to load their firearms.

Going Hot! I start my live fire drills with some basic close-in targets in the same manner as the previous empty gun practice above. Typically the targets used have minimum detail and are bottle shaped. The intent here is to not visually overload the student at this point in the program. Keep the round counts low at first as this allows you to make immediate corrections as needed. Don't expect the same level of shooting skills observed during daylight range activities. The stress of shooting in the dark and the added burden of learning to coordinate the firearm in conjunction with the light will cause scores to drop. Try hard to develop a rhythm to the exercises. You'll find this helps the staff and students alike.

As the students start to gain some confidence and skill, the exercises should become more complicated. Challenge them with more complex realistic targets, reactive targets, movement, and multiple targets. Allow only one shooter at a time forward of the firing line during the more complex drills that require shooters to aggress targets down range. To force visual patience, constantly change the images of the targets. Replace guns with cell phones, knives with pens, badges with weapons and anything else to force them to really assess the suspect. Throughout all these exercises increase the verbal interaction of your students. I want my students directing and controlling their suspects with all methods available to them. Their verbal direction and overall communication is a vital part of all the exercises.

Like in the force on force drills, make sure that all the live fire drills do not turn into a shoot situation. We must strive to force the student into as many decision making processes while under stress as possible. This decision making process can be complicated beyond the shoot don't shoot scenario by adding a where to shoot consideration. I can often tell which of my students has had SWAT training or experience by the manner they handle one of my exercises in particular. The exercise requires the student to move laterally across the firing line while aggressing a number of targets. These targets are a mix of shoot and no shoot situations. As these targets are encountered the student must assess threat or no threat and to shoot or not to shoot.

One of the bad guy targets I use is a thug dressed in dark clothing pointing a gun at the student. This is a unique target as he is wearing a ballistic vest. It is this element that allows me further insight into the student's visual patience and previous tactical training. I find almost without exception that the students who shoot this target in the head and not center mass into the ballistic vest are SWAT or have had SWAT training. Very few of the students will recognize that the center mass shot may not be the best choice and alter their point of aim.

What does this say about how we are training our patrol personnel with respect to critical decision making and visual patience? I'll let you come to your own conclusion. I believe you should structure some of your drills and exercises to reinforce the principles of visual patience and critical decision making. Put your own twist on it and tailor the drills to your agency's particular circumstances.

If your facilities allow, try to alter the levels of light the students are exposed to throughout the range period. In my own facility I am blessed with the ability to create total darkness, moonlight, streetlight, and any level in between. In addition, I have a light bar mounted on a dolly that allows me to position the light anywhere on the range. This light bar is on an adjustable pole that allows for SUV or patrol car height adjustments. I also use a siren to add the ambient noise issues as well. I also play tapes of radio traffic and suspect dialog during some of the live fire scenarios.

A realistic training environment is something you should always strive for in your training. However, never compromise safety for realism. Low-light training should be programmed into your annual training schedule. I have found that attendance at low-light ranges is always better if they are scheduled well in advance. Get the support of your administration to the point that they attend all your range dates. I believe low-light training should be conducted on a quarterly basis with qualification conducted semi-annually.

Diversity in your training curriculum is critical to keeping your students motivated. I include the qualification course in every range outing. Sometimes it is obviously the qualification course and other times the stages are dispersed into the shooting scenarios. The bottom line is to get the students shooting and practicing the skill sets needed to successfully pass the qualification course of fire.

Design your courses of fire to challenge the students to try different light and firearm techniques. Keep them working on developing their own specific light and firearm system. Encourage them to incorporate multiple light techniques throughout your scenarios. They will soon find what works for them and gain confidence in their abilities. You will see the improvement in their scores and in the time or efficiency demonstrated performing the tasks you have assigned.

Speaking of scores, keep good records. Regardless of the effort required, develop a system that is equitable to the students but defendable to the administration. The scores and performance standards will help you assess the effectiveness of your program. They are discoverable in litigation situations and could very well be the saving grace for you, your students, or your agency.

Keep your training Real
Remember Popow

Popow v. City of Margate New Jersey is often called the "Failure To Train" case. This case from the late 1970's was filed under Title 42, Section 1983, of the U.S. Civil Rights Act. The court ruled that a failure to conduct realistic firearms training, specifically low-light firing, can constitute negligence by the department.

"I hear, I forget; I see, I remember;
I do, I understand"

Confucius

You will fight the way you train. How often have we heard that? I believe the most dynamic method of training for refinement of skill sets and validation of understanding is the scenario based Force on Force (FOF) training model (also known as Reality Based Training). I will do my best to explain how to use FOF in your training programs. Anyone who needs a deeper understanding of this training method should read Ken Murray's book titled "<u>Training at the Speed of Life</u>". I strongly recommend you purchase Ken's book as it is packed with critical information that you will use beyond the scope of Reality Based Training. I consider Ken's book the authority for all my reality based training. My programs are better, the safety of my staff and students is never compromised, and the learning process is uncomplicated because I follow the recommendations in Ken's book. Don't ever pass up an opportunity to attend any of Ken's lectures, seminars or training courses if Reality Based Training is of interest to you.

Force on Force scenario training is not to be taken lightly. I believe you lose immeasurable value in this type of training if not conducted properly. To merely set role players in motion without proper preparation and council can be dangerous and counter productive.

Students moving through FOF exercise

Let's discuss the safety considerations of reality based training before going any further. There is so much more to be concerned with than just the four primary rules of firearm safety. Even though you will be using simulation guns, never allow any violations of the four basic rules. In addition, set up a Secured

Safety Zone that is closely monitored. The Safety Zone is a controlled area that is posted with signs that identify the area and list the rules.

Do not allow any live weapons or live ammunition in the Safety Zone at any time. I even use a hand held metal detector to ensure nothing slips past the pat-down. No one is ever allowed to enter the Safety Zone without a thorough search by at least two safety officers.

Make it clear to everyone participating in the exercises that anyone can call a "cease fire". All of my safety officers and staff are equipped with a whistle to call an immediate end to any activity. Instruct all participants to call a cease fire immediately if they experience any type of safety equipment failure. No student is ever expected or asked to do anything they are not comfortable attempting. Make it a point of asking all your participants to disclose any injuries or training limitations.

Do not allow any horseplay or unsafe behavior in or around the training area and require protective equipment be worn by all participants and spectators during all training activities.

My scenarios are strictly controlled. My role players must stick to their script and I absolutely refuse any adlibbing on their part. Every scenario has a specific learning point. I have written scripts for my role players to read and refer to during the scenario. Many role players will take a quick peek at them while they are waiting for the initial contact with the officers/students and the exercise to really get going. It is important to have a master plan as well as a balanced understanding of how reality based training can facilitate your training objective.

Ken says in his book <u>Training at the Speed of Life</u>, "You Don't Know What You Don't Know". I believe people often make dangerous assumptions based on incomplete or incorrect information. Do not allow this to happen to you as you begin to develop a reality based training program. Take the time to research every aspect of your FOF scenario based training program. As you put your lesson plan together, account for every experience level of student you may encounter. Use a building block (crawl before you walk, walk before you run) system in your FOF scenarios. I find this progressive format allows the students to recognize their limitations and immediately begin to work on implementing corrections to these shortfalls. Whether they admit it or not, many students experience high levels of anxiety when participating in FOF training. My programs allow for this by exposing them to similar scenarios in succession before they move on to more challenging exercises. This progressive format and the immediate critique and after action review seem to be the most productive.

Guard against developing scenarios that are not realistic. Every exercise you put the students through must be plausible. Try to use realistic settings, props, and current equipment. I am very fortunate when training at my home base that I have access to a 30,000 square foot warehouse. This building has two floors, three stairwells and the diversity in room configurations one would expect from a building this size. In fact, I will often conduct an entire day of FOF exercises in complete darkness. I will often tell the students "if you can do it in the dark you can do it in the light". However that is not my primary motivation. The darkness adds an unbelievable level of stress to most of my students. I have witnessed the most grounded of operators second guess themselves in the darken environment.

Students during FOF training in the dark

As in the real world, make sure that all the scenarios don't end with the need for lethal force. In fact, if shooting is necessary, take the scenario beyond the bad guy going down. You can incorporate the aftermath of a shooting based on your agency's policies, apprehension/custody issues, first aid procedures, crime scene security, etc. Your exercises should allow the students to implement the use of force continuum. Challenge their interpretation of their agency's policies and procedures.

Recently I have added more communication requirements into my scenarios. This includes the communication between the team members during the exercise and the team's communications with command and control elements, other LE agencies, K9, and Emergency Medical Services. Again the addition of this element has increased the overall realism and increased the level of anxiety among the participants. You may even want to create an audio or video recording of the exercises. These tapes will prove to be the source of much discussion during the overall after action review of the day's activities.

Just a few final thoughts on developing FOF scenarios. I believe you need to test your scenarios before you expose your students to them. You need to guard against the possible unanticipated student response. A test run or scenario evaluation will hopefully bring out any shortfalls. If you are not getting the responses you anticipated, resist the desire to control or influence the student's actions during the exercise.

Build trust between you and your students. In Ken's book he says, "allow your students the courage to fail". Establish an environment in which your students know when all is said and done they will have identified what needs to be reprogrammed to guarantee improved performance in future encounters.

A Few Words On Equipment:

You have a number of options as you evaluate simulated weapons systems for your Force on Force training. Everything from paintball to Simunitions™, to Air Soft is readily available. I use Air Soft equipment because it is very cost effective and your training can be very realistic if you use high-end guns.

The brand of gun that has proven to be very realistic in function, weight and feel, is made by a company called KWA. These guns are very accurate and hold up very well to abuse. These higher end guns are almost always green gas operated. Don't skimp on the green gas. The green gas is a little more expensive than other gases. However, the green gas has a silicon additive that keeps your guns running smoothly. The magazines like all air soft magazines are very fragile. They will work great as long as you don't do combat reloads or drop the magazines.

These guns will fit in the like holster for the real gun they are modeled after. In addition, most if not all your accessories (lights and lasers) will fit the air soft guns as well. I do not allow my students to load their air soft magazines beyond the capacity of their real guns. This ensures they have a sense of the need to reload or at least a more realistic knowledge of how long their magazines will last in a real gun fight.

I use black colored air soft ammo in all my scenarios. I do this to eliminate the possibility of the student seeing the trajectory of the incoming rounds. Even though my air soft guns are operating at well over 300 ft per second some students claim they are able to see the white ammo as it is shot in their direction. Again this is trying to keep the training as real as possible.

I provide full 360 degree head and face protection to all my students during FOF training. Many people opt for the face protection and don't worry much about the back of the head. This is not acceptable by my standards. Our scenarios are very realistic and one can never assume the angle or direction of the shot will always be face first.

I encourage my students not to wear their ballistic vest during air soft training. I want the student to feel the impact of the air soft ammo just as they would a real bullet. This eliminates the arguing that we sometimes see in FOF training when someone says "I hit you" and the other says "No you did not".

All in all, the high end air soft equipment has worked well for me. My students love it and can't get enough of this type of training. Choose your FOF equipment carefully and be creative in its use. Your program and you will be better off due to your efforts.

*"When DEATH is the alternative,
INJURY has its appeal".*

A POW FROM THE VIETNAM WAR

Thinking out of the box is a statement that has been overused to the point of saturation for most of us. But in our world it is a concept that is not without merit. As you have read the previous chapters, I hope you were able to see that my approach to low-light shooting is based more on what works today than what may have been presented to us in years past. As technology advances and practitioners continue to push the envelope our performance capabilities and overall security continue to improve.

This chapter is intended to present for your consideration, a number of alternative lighting systems, accessories and specific equipment that you may find helpful. Here we will discuss alternative lighting systems, night sights, laser devices, and miscellaneous accessories.

Before we discuss alternative lighting systems and accessories, let's look at night sights and laser devices. When operating in the low-light environment finding traditional iron sights can be very difficult. Add a level of stress to this scenario and getting proper sight alignment becomes almost impossible. Self-luminous (night sights) provide a significant advantage to the operator when trying to establish a sight picture in the dark.   In total darkness without the advantage of night sights I have difficulty seeing my sights, my gun and even my hands for that matter. I installed night sights on a couple of my air soft guns for use during my force on force training scenarios. The students with the night sight equipped guns routinely achieve a higher hit ratio.

Night sights are not the panacea solution or end all fix to seeing your sights in the dark. There are some negative aspects of their use that we need to consider.

During the BAR as discussed earlier, we can assume the operator will have both eyes open as he concentrates on the threat. Michael Conti, author of a must read book titled <u>Police Pistolcraft</u>, points out that "when under stressful situations such as a gunfight, self-luminous sights may be a distraction or impede the shooter's focus from the threat".   Given the forced two eye vision during extreme stress, the shooter may experience greater confusion especially if trained to close one eye during range exercises. He may see multiple sight posts or dots or even a blurry image of the sights.

There are a number of solutions to these considerations. Some operators will select night sights with the front sight a different color from the rear sight in hopes of maintaining front and rear sight perspective. Some shooters prefer a self-luminous front sight only. I have self-luminous sights on my duty Sig220. I chose a self-luminous front sight in the shape of a dot and a self-luminous dash shape for the rear. With this configuration, I just put the circle over the dash and I am certain of the alignment.

It seems like we can never stock enough laser sights in our retail pro shop at our training center. They are one of the most popular accessories we sell. The appeal of these devices seems to be universal among armed citizens and armed professionals. Crimson Trace™ and LaserMax® are without a doubt the most asked for versions of laser aiming devices.

My students often ask my opinion on the use of laser aiming devices. I tell them that I believe they have application for the untrained shooter and the advanced shooter but for very different reasons.

The untrained shooter when faced with a threat will most likely focus on the threat. As they are so focused on the threat they will forget everything they learned about sight alignment, sight picture, trigger control and most everything else associated with shooting a hand gun accurately. Under these circumstances, the shooter will clearly see the red dot of the laser projected on the threat. If the gun were fired the bullet would impact where the red dot is projected.

While attending the ILEETA conference last year I participated in a discussion concerning laser aiming devices. One of the concerns expressed by one instructor from the Midwest was that he had witnessed shooters not shooting as soon as they needed to because the could not find the red dot on the target. Any hesitation to shoot when the shot is necessary must be corrected.

This hesitation factor should be considered during your training sessions. The shooter must not be conditioned to shoot only when the dot is visible. Creative training scenarios and courses of fire must be established and mastered by the student to ensure desired performance in the field.   As with any tool or device, we as trainers must establish programs that allow our students to master the equipment and not become dependent on it.

As a firearms instructor I am sometimes at a loss in trying to determine if the student understands sight alignment and sight picture. After all, in some cases the bullet holes in the paper are no indication of the students understanding. I use a technique I picked up while attending a Crimson Trace training course we hosted at my facility.

I direct the student to take up a good two handed shooting position and aim at the center of the bullseye. While they are doing this I cover the laser on the firearm they are aiming. When the student is sure they are on target and have a good sight picture, I remove my finger from the laser opening. The laser beam is then projected at the point of aim. If the dot is on the bullseye, I know the student understands the concept. If not then we have our work cut out for us.

When evaluating laser aiming systems to stock in my pro shop I considered LaserMax® and Crimson Trace™. I decided on Crimson Trace based on their design, function and performance. The Crimson Trace lasers are a grip replacement or grip attachment configuration. This is very appealing to me as it does not require the replacement of any major functional parts of the handgun.

The Crimson Trace laser grips will not affect the function or operation of the hand gun. They are very durable, unobtrusive and allow the weapon to be holstered in its original equipment. The pressure activated switches are located in the grip panels and for the most part are passively activated. In that regard I mean that when you grip the handgun with your dominate hand you activate the laser. This is a plus for the novice shooter but may be a concern for an operator who may prefer intermittent use of the laser. This issue is easily resolved for most shooters through training and practice. In most cases I have found that by altering your grip or the pressure applied by the grip you can effectively control switching the laser on/off.

Practice is also the solution for the first finger blocking the laser beam while the finger is up along the frame in the index (off trigger) position. A slight adjustment of your normal index position is often all that is necessary to correct this problem.

The Crimson Trace laser grip system comes with two very small Allen wrenches that allow you to adjust the sight for windage and elevation. I have found these adjustments to be very stable and have not experienced any issues with losing zero. Follow the manufacturer's direction for setting the zero. The laser is located on the right side of the handgun and typically above the bore of the handgun. This causes the zero to be very distance sensitive. Because the laser beam is projected at an angle to the bore it will eventually intersect the path of the bullet and project on the opposite side of the bore line. Depending on the distance, this offset between red dot and bullet impact point can range from insignificant to a number of inches.

Because of this variable of beam alignment and bullet impact at various distances, I do not recommend you attempt a critical precision shot using only the laser.

The LaserMax® system is a replacement of the pistol's guide rod. To install the laser you remove the stock recoil spring and guide rod and replace those parts with the supplied LaserMax components. On some model pistols you may need to replace the takedown lever and replace it with one supplied by LaserMax. Functional reliability is a major concern for any firearm used for defense. Therefore, I have stayed away from any accessories that require the removal or replacement of stock components.

One of the most useful light systems for use after the scene is secure is the headlamp. A powerful headlamp will prove to be an invaluable tool when you are searching for evidence or surveying a crime scene. The obvious advantage is that you have full use of both hands. All headlamps are not created equal so evaluate them as you would any other piece of equipment. The headlamps I am talking about here are not of the variety we grew up with.

LED technology and smaller power sources allow us color options, brightness, beam quality, and wearing comfort never before experienced in headlamps. I prefer the style that allows the wearer to adjust the beam angle. I also use the multiple color option in many ways.

When trying to preserve my night vision, I will often use a red or green LED beam. These colors allow me to see clearly without exposing my eyes to more light than is necessary. If you are a hunter you will love the color LED feature for walking into your hunting sight before the sun comes up.

My favorite headlamp is the eGear K2-Focus. The K2 features a revolutionary Focus Control LED which allows you to adjust the light beam from Spot to Flood. The K2 LED projects an 85 Lumen clean white light. I especially like the Red, Blue, and Green light capability of this model. You will find these color options very useful when trying to conserve battery life or attempting to preserve your night vision.

The water resistant K2 is equipped with a slim unobtrusive battery pack that features a red rear LED for safety. It features an instant off switch that works in any lighting mode. Operational modes include an on/off High and Low beam in the flashing or constant on mode. The red, green, and blue LED's work in constant on or flashing modes as well. The rear red light located on the battery pack features a constant on/off or flashing mode.

The K2 is powered by 3 AA batteries with rated burn time between 16 hours and 500 hours depending on the mode of operation. The system weighs 5 oz. with batteries installed.

Streamlight's Sidewinder

Another option for an alternative lighting source is the Streamlight Sidewinder™. The Sidewinder is one of the most versatile lighting systems I have ever seen. The folks at Streamlight say the Sidewinder is 20 flashlights in one. I have never taken the time to count, so let's take their word for it. Each LED features 4 levels of output intensities: Low (5%), Medium (20%), Medium-High (50%), High (100%) plus a Strobe function (100%).

It has one switch for On-Off, dimming and mode selection functions. The color selector knob is a pull-to-turn locking rotary selector with tactile indicator for easy operation with gloves. A double click button allows you to initiate strobe function from "Off" position. Variable output levels of the light from the off position are accomplished with a push and hold button.

The unit is powered by 2 AA batteries. Burn time ranges from 1 hour to 100 hours depending on the mode and power level of operation selected.   Keeping with the all weather/rugged condition capabilities of this light it will also accept 2 AA lithium batteries, which allow extended operation, or extreme temperatures (-40°F - 150°F).   The High-impact, super-tough nylon case drop-test verified from 30 feet easily mounts to MOLLE or ACH for hands-free use.

Sidewinder's Rotating Head

A couple of features that have proven very helpful to me are the tethered tailcap which has kept me from losing it during night operations. The articulating 185° rotating head provides you with a plethora of options. The unit weighs just under 5 oz and is available in Coyote Tan and Marine Olive Drab.

As accessories go, don't overlook the importance of making the proper light holster selection. Regardless of which brand or model of flashlight you choose you should have a holster that is comfortable, durable and allows for secure carry and easy access to the light.   I am not a big fan of the snap flat security type of holster. I prefer the Kydex variety that allows for an easy draw stroke of the light. As you evaluate the holsters available, look for one that will allow you to present the light in a smooth fluid motion in conjunction with your firearm. You should be able to deploy the light with your support hand only. An added benefit would be a holster that allowed for light access by either hand.

I prefer a bezel down configuration. This is especially true when using a smaller tactical light. You are capable of establishing the grips required for many of the light techniques with a bezel down holstered light configuration. One of my favorite light holster manufacturers is a Northwest company called Holsters Plus. They are a small company that is rapidly gaining popularity across the country. The products are top quality and lifetime guaranteed.

In conclusion, it is not my intent to promote any specific brand, model, or type of equipment. I have mentioned specifics on a number of pieces of equipment throughout this book. These are items that I have personal experience with and I felt it necessary to share my experiences with you. There are many manufacturers producing quality equipment for you to use.

I encourage you to try them all and experiment, investigate and evaluate them on their particular merits. Make an informed decision as you choose your tools and your training as well. When you find something that works, don't be shy... Share it with the rest of us. Thank You...

Low-light Power Point Sample

This low-light power point is provided as an example to assist you in the development of your own presentation. It is one of the presentations I use in my low-light training. In the interest of space and volume, I have omitted the photos that normally accompany this document. I encourage you to add any images that may assist your students in understanding this information. As you go through these slides realize that many of them do not contain statements that are complete thoughts. They have been developed to act more as a tickler/outline for me to expand upon during my lecture. Feel free to copy, change, rearrange the slide order or modify this information in any way necessary to support your training efforts.

Presentation Outline

- Day One
  - Overview
  - Light in the tactical world
  - Light and your eyes
  - Rods and Cones
  - Low-Light Human Effects
  - Emotions of Shooting & Visual Patience
  - Equipment Essentials
  - Equipment Techniques
  - Light as a "Force Option"
  - Movement with light
  - Live Fire range
- Day Two
  - Force on Force Simulation Scenarios

Tactical World
The Importance of Light

- 70 LE killed in 2001 (not counting 9/11)
- 60% killed during hours of darkness
- 83% killed within 20' and 2.5 seconds
- Most within 2 minutes of arriving on scene

YOU NEED BOTH TECHNIQUE AND PRINCIPLE UNDERSTANDING TO BE MOST EFFECTIVE..

Tactical World
The Importance of Light

Operators who know how to control their environment and their suspect with light will drastically improve their chances of surviving and prevailing in a low-light lethal force encounter.

Tactical World
The Importance of Light

Effective Low-Light tactics can only be accomplished with:

- Top quality equipment
- Through cutting-edge training
- Practice Practice Practice

Low-Light Facts

- Every 13 years the amount of light a person needs to see in Low-Light doubles
  - *This means @ 45 you need 4 times as much light as you did @ 19*
- The eyes' ability to focus peaks @ age 10
  - *It begins to decline while you are in your mid to late 20's*

Light and Your Eyes

- Starlight = <1/2 moon No direct light
  - During First 2 min = 20/800 = < 5%
  - After 12 min = 20/300 = 15%
  - After 30 min = 20/200 Legally impaired

Light and Your Eyes

What you see is determined by the existing light combined with the perceived expectations of the brain

- Often only receive snapshots
- Low-light breeds Target Fixation (TV)

Rods and Cones

- **Retina** – made of 2 types of neuroreceptors
  - Rods
    - Located primarily in periphery
    - Low-Light = they take over pick up peripheral vision
      - Pick up movement
      - Detect potential threats, not ID them
      - It's why visual info is severely degraded in low-light
  - Cones
    - Located primarily in center
    - Sufficient light = depth, color, fine detail

Negative Effects

- Most Pronounced = Bright to Dark
  - Movie = typically 20/800
  - 4 X's as bad as Legally Blind threshold
- Eye Will Adapt
  - Rods develop light sensitive chemical
  - Rhodopsin makes rods more responsive

Negative Effects

- Full Darkness Adaptation Process
  - L to D – Takes approximately 40 minutes
  - 12 minutes – 20/300 15% visual efficiency
  - 25LUX (just above candle) wpn vs object ?

  D to L = Almost immediate

Negative Effects

- Field of Vision Blind Spot Center
  - Cones nonfunctioning = Blind Spot
- Off Center Viewing
  - Allows for greater threat ID
  - Especially if moving

Negative Effects

- Binocular Viewing
  - Keep both eyes open
  - Provides approximately 2½ times visual sensitivity
- Ability to Adapt
  - Iris = control pupil size less flexible w/age
  - Good Fitness = blood flow = better adaptation
  - Caffeine, Nicotine, Alcohol = reduced adaptation
- Self Help
  - Wear sunglasses, Vitamin A (Caution Toxic)

Comfort Zone

- Rule the Night
    - Like anything else familiarity breeds confidence
    - Darkness must become a familiar environment
    - You must be confident
    - Adrenaline dump = dilates pupils = poor vision
- The Legal Standard
    - Your vision is diminished = Not the legal Std

Emotions Of Shooting

- Personal Comfort Zone
    - Your mind trying to appease your body
- Natural Flinch
    - Flinch/defensive mechanisms for a minute
    - Train mind to immediately take control
    - You must progress quickly & violently to your offensive tactics

Emotions Of Shooting

- Aggression (Controlled)
  - Don't just point the weapon…Drive it to the target
  - Move… don't waste precious time
- Suspect Dictates UOF
  - Easier to reduce LOF than to ramp it up
  - Ramping up LOF takes time

Visual Patience

- In crisis, your mind cannot perceive you are doing things fast enough
- Mind – Literally *screaming* at you to move faster
- You must fight to control these emotions in order to maintain VP
- You must proceed based on your learned tactics

Target Assessment

- Target type
  - Hard or Soft
  - Stationary or Moving
- Target Environment
  - Indoors, outside, collateral damage
- Number of targets
  - Tactical ops??   - battle plan – rules of eng

Light Utilization

- **Movement** – Your navigation
- **Search** - Open up the darkness
- **Identification** – Confirm what your "mind" sees
- **Control** – Hot spot? Direct & Control Suspect's Movements
- **Signaling** – As a pointer or use clock face with como

Equipment Essentials

- Handheld or Weapons mounted
  - High-Output beam
  - Switch methods
  - Power
  - Accessory hardware

Equipment Techniques

Low Light Principles
- Assess the environment
- Limit Backlighting
- Don't use more light than you need
- Light & move off the LOA
- Intermittent use
  - Displacements – Vertical, Horizontal, & Distance
  - Angle of beam
  - Rhythm and Duration

Equipment Techniques

- Anticipate suspect's reaction
- Dominate with light
- Have a backup and spare batteries

Terminology

- Hand Confusion
  - Often under high stress conditions
  - Hands intended for separate tasks
- Light/Hold Displacement
  - With or without gun & light together
  - Desired point of illumination is not on target
- Low-Light Conditions
  - Diminished light inside of structure or outdoors
  - Normally associated with dark shadows and lack of uniform light
- Sympathetic Contraction
  - Contraction of all digits – most often when startled

Common Handheld Options

- Harries
- Rogers/SureFire
- Ayoob
- FBI/Modified FBI
- Neck Index
- Hargreaves Technique
- Keller Technique
- USMC Technique
- Over/Under Technique

Harries

- Named after Michael Harries
- Uses an "Ice pick grip"
- Backs of hands = isometric tension

Tactical
Services Group
A Division of Center Target Sports, Inc.

Harries

Pros
▪Works well with large or small lights
▪Two hands on the gun
▪Works well with Weaver stance

Cons
▪Beam displacement
▪Light located @ shooters center of mass
▪Possible muzzle sweeping

Tactical
Services Group
A Division of Center Target Sports, Inc.

Rogers/SureFire

▪Dev. by former FBI agent Bill Rogers
▪Close to normal shooting grip
▪Syringe grip with tail cap switch
▪Modified by SureFire to work with their
"Syringe" grip light

Rogers/SureFire

Pros
- Rapid deployment from holster
- Good beam alignment
- Two handed support position

Cons
- Needs a small light with push tail cap
- Sympathetic contraction = AD
- Light located @ shooters center mass

Ayoob Technique

- Developed by Massad Ayoob
- Best suited for quick / unprepared presentation
- Not advisable for long distance shooting

Ayoob Technique

- Pros
    - Works from normal sword grip
    - Can be held close-in easy movement
- Cons
    - Works only with side switch flashlight
    - Fatiguing
    - Weapon tends to bang light
    - Light is located center mass

FBI/Modified FBI

- Spear or Ice pick grip
- Light held at arms reach and forward
- Possibly the "oldest" light technique
- Once believed to be outdated but the modified version is gaining popularity
- Modification = aggressive unpredictable movement

FBI/Modified FBI

Pros
- Works with large and small lights
- Allows searching without muzzle sweep
- Peripheral light illuminates sights and target

Cons
- Limits shooter to one hand
- Practice needed to maintain light and muzzle alignment
- Can be fatiguing

Neck Index

- SureFire Instructors Ken Good & Dave Maynard
- Modified the flashlight on shoulder technique for better application of the smaller tactical light

Neck Index

Pros
- Works with small or large lights
- Allows simultaneous illumination of sights/target
- Allows for searching without muzzle sweep
- Natural position for striking with light

Cons
- Limits user to one handed shooting
- Can draw fire to users head
- Can create excess flash on back
 of weapon

Hargreaves Technique

- Named after Mike Hargreaves of the British Army
- Introduced in 2002
- Tail cap light pushed against GH knuckles

Hargreaves Technique

- Pros
  - Easy to learn
  - Keeps beam aligned W/barrel
  - Allows for steadier two hand shooting
- Cons
  - Does not work W/side button light
  - Difficult to use with injured hand
  - Light is located center mass

Keller Technique

- Named after Van Keller of the Georgia State Police
- Variation of the Harries technique
- Uses light-over hand

Keller Technique

- Pros
  - Light is fairly well aligned W/barrel
  - Enables steadier two handed shooting
- Cons
  - Does not work W/side button light
  - Difficult to use with injured hand
  - Light is located center mass

USMC Technique

- Developed by the Embassy Guard school at the USMC training center VA
- Sword grip W/side mount switch
- Light Basel Rim pressed against fingers of gun hand
- Create stabilizing tension

USMC Technique

- Pros
  - Very comfortable
  - Good light/barrel alignment
  - Enables steadier two hand shooting
- Cons
  - Works only W/side switch light
  - Barrel/beam displacement common on discharge
  - Sympathetic discharge possible with hand confusion
  - Light is located at center mass

Over/Under Technique

- Originated within the New York City PD
- Sword grip
- Side mounted switch
- Weapon hand pressed down firmly on light hand
- Firm isometric tension

Over/Under Technique

- Pros
  - Works with small or large lights
  - Good beam/barrel alignment
  - Fairly usable with injured hand or arm
- Cons
  - Works only W/side switch light
  - Sympathetic discharge issue
  - Light located at center mass

Light as a Force Option

- What are force options?
- Have you ever used force options?
- Gain compliance or desired suspect action with minimum use of force

Light as a Force Option

- Some examples...

Movement with Light
OODA Loop

Korean Air War
- Mig Jet faster than US Jet
- US Jet more maneuverable, tighter loop
- US Jet, chased, could loop around and come up behind enemy Jet

Concept = get inside adversary's OODA loop process to WIN

Observe.........Orient.........Decide.........Act

Movement with Light

Academia	OODA Loop
Perception	Observe
Evaluation	Orient
Decision	Decide
Action	Act

Movement with Light

One Man Cornering

- Position off the corner and start as early as possible
- Slice the pie
- Displace vertically with each slice
- If suspect is engaged try not to retreat unless absolutely necessary

Movement with Light

One Man Doorway Cornering
- Begin as far away and as early as possible
- Slice the pie (vary the pace)
- If suspect is engaged try not to retreat unless absolutely necessary

Movement with Light

Team Movement
- Keep separation
- Threat is presented = Team displaces to force threat to split focus
- Team movements can = a Force multiplier

Movement with Light

Fatal Funnel
- ■Criss-Cross High Low
    - ■Crouch - initiates movement
    - ■Standing - follows and extends weapon over partner's back entering room at same instant controlling his half of the room
    - ■Neither officer is ever exposed as both move under cover and quickly out of FF

THANK YOU

Any Questions?

Low-Light Training

Tactical Services Group
P.O. Box 2487
Hayden, ID 83835
www.tacticalservicesgroup.com   (author's program)

SureFire Institute
18300 Mount Baldy Circle
Fountain Valley, CA 92708

Recommended Reading

Books:

Stress Fire
By: Massad Ayoob

In the Gravest Extreme
By: Massad Ayoob

The Farnam Method of Defensive Handgunning
By: John Farnam

The Street Smart Gun Book
By: John Farnam

Training at the Speed of Life
By: Ken Murray

Police Pistolcraft
By: Michael E. Conti

On Killing
Lt. Colonel Dave Grossman

Secrets of a Master Gunfighter
Jim Cirillo

Tactical Anatomy
By: Dr. James Williams

Clinical research:

Vision and Shooting
By: Dr. Edward Godnig

Biological Limits of Police Combat Handgun Shooting Accuracy
B. Vila and G. Morrison
American Journal of Police, Volume 13, No. 1, 1994

Dry fire practice is often a recommendation of mine to students experiencing handgun manipulation problems. Most often I recommend dry fire exercises to improve trigger press and recoil anticipation issues.

For the purposes of this book I want to offer for your consideration Dry Fire Practice to improve your flashlight handgun manipulation skills. I want you to use dry fire practice to develop and perfect your flashlight techniques.

As in all dry fire exercises, Safety must be the primary concern. I never dry fire practice in the same room with real ammunition. I always dry fire practice when I am alone for maximum concentration. Below are the Safety Procedures I follow every time I begin a dry fire practice session:

- Establish a practice area and make sure it is free of any live ammunition.
- Try to insure your privacy when selecting a practice area. Possibly lock a door or post the area with a no ammunition allowed sign.
- Clear your firearm and all magazines of live ammunition.
- Establish an appropriate backstop for the caliber firearm in use.
- Unlike dry fire practice for shooting skill improvement, I want you to place a LARGE lifelike target in front of the backstop.
- Double and triple check that your firearm is clear and safe.

As you begin to practice, make sure all your movements are realistic. Train as you will fight. Do not take any short cuts. As you present the firearm in conjunction with the flashlight, do it with a purpose. Make every effort to stay true to the techniques you are trying to master. Wear your duty gear or carry your equipment as you normally would.

Concentrate on the bore/beam alignment. Pay particular attention to the hot spot of the light beam. As you are using a lifelike silhouette target, practice placing the hot spot in the eyes of the target while maintaining the appropriate sight picture with the firearm.

Take advantage of these dry fire sessions and practice recovering from firearm stoppages while using the flashlight. A recovery procedure as simple as Tap, Rack, Bang can be very challenging when you add the firearm to the process. The important thing to keep in mind is practice as many scenarios as possible and become familiar with the skills necessary for you to perform your chosen techniques safely and effectively.

BOOK QUICK ORDER FORM

Postal Orders: Tactical Services Group
                            P. O. Box 2487
                            Hayden, Idaho 83835

Website Orders: www.tacticalservicesgroup.com

Please send me _________ copies of:

Rule the Night – Win the Fight
        A practical guide to low-light gunfighting

Price: $19.95 (+ 5.95 Shipping U.S.) Total Cost: $25.90

Orders Shipped to Idaho addresses ONLY add 6.00% Sales Tax: $1.20

For total cost of: $27.10

I have enclosed a check or money order for $ _____________

Ship to:

Name: ____

Address: ____

City: _______________________________State_____________ Zip_____________

Phone: ____________________________Email:_______________________________

Shipping & Handling Costs:

U.S. $5.95
International: $12.00

Postal Orders: Please send check or money order made out to Tactical Services Group.

Please note: Copies of this book are available at special discounts for bulk purchase.